POWER UP YOUR PEOPLE SKILLS: COMMUNICATING IN THE NEW MILLENNIUM

Doug Malouf

Business & Professional Publishing

Published by Business & Professional Publishing
Unit 7/5 Vuko Place
Warriewood NSW 2102 Australia

First published as *Switch on Your Magnetic Personality* 1993.

New edition published as *Power Up Your People Skills* 1998.

The National Library of Australia
Cataloguing-in-Publication entry

Malouf, Doug.
    Power up your people skills: communicating in the new millennium.
    Rev. ed.
    ISBN 1 875680 71 3.
    1. Self-esteem. 2. Public speaking. 3. Oral communication. 4. Personality development.
    5. Written communication. I. Title.
808.5

10 9 8 7 6 5 4 3 2 1

Edited by Jane Angus
Series design by Kim Webber
Formatting and paging by Lauren Statham, Alice Graphics
Printed and bound in Australia by Australian Print Group

Distribution in Australia by Woodslane Pty Ltd. Business & Professional Publishing books are available through booksellers and other resellers across Australia and New Zealand. For further information contact Woodslane Pty Ltd on ph (02) 9970 5111, fax (02) 9970 5002 or e-mail info@woodslane.com.au

CONTENTS

ABOUT THE AUTHOR

Doug Malouf is described by his peers as one of the most innovative and inventive presenters in the world of corporate communicators. He has authored 8 best selling books, 5 audio cassette programs and his company DTS International now works with 25000 people a year on the world wide training circuit. You can visit his website at *www.dougspeak.com* or you can email him at *dtstraining@bigpond.com*.

Doug can be contacted at:

DTS International

54 Flinders Street
Darlinghurst NSW 2010
Telephone: (02) 9360 5111
Facsimile: (02) 9360 5199

Visit our Website at www.dougspeak.com

PREFACE

I spend a large amount of my time travelling around conducting seminars, so naturally I meet a great many people. I always notice those who project an air of natural self-confidence. 'Another great people person' I find myself thinking, watching the effect they have on others around them. They do more than light up a room—they stand out like beacons.

I notice, too, those who seem to have difficulty with communication skills. They range from efficient, accomplished business professionals to 'quiet achievers'. When I talk to such people, I find that, much as they would dearly love to project their 'real' selves to others, they can't. They have never learnt the simple steps to gaining self-confidence and mastering the art of true communication.

Why is it that some people relate instinctively to others, while others avoid the limelight and desperately wish they knew the secret of effortless communication? I have always found the differences intriguing. And the more I delved into the causes, the more I became convinced it was time to write a book on the subject.

Really, there is no big secret to developing powerful people skills. First you need to understand your basic personality type, and what it is about you that makes you interesting and different—and make no mistake, we are all interesting and different in some way. Then it's a matter of learning to project that unique personality, so you can relate well to others. In short, it's all about mastering communication skills.

The rewards for spending time on learning to project your personality are great—personally, socially and professionally. No longer will you have to sit back, wondering where others get their confidence from and how to relate to people generally. You, too, will possess those powerful people skills—skills that are there, just waiting for you to have the confidence to use them!

Special thanks to Margaret McAlister for her writing skills, to Monique and Tim at Woodslane for putting it all together, to Allan Stomann for his excellent illustrations and to my staff, Janice, Julie and Simon. And of course to you, the reader, for having enough confidence in me to buy this book.

Stay positive!

Doug

INTRODUCTION

WHAT ARE 'PEOPLE SKILLS'?

The foundation stone of any successful career or business is effective human interaction. Or, to put it as plainly as possible, people skills.

This is not a new idea, but it is becoming more important than ever before. The business world has changed dramatically in the past decade, and it continues to change. Companies have downsized, work patterns have altered, tenure of employment is a thing of the past. More and more people are starting small business operations, and many are working from home.

Whether you're building a career working for others or starting your own business, you need to make a commitment to your own personal development. It's no good looking forlornly at your boss or lecturer or mentor and expecting them to take that responsibility. They've got their own careers to think about.

Now that the new millennium is upon us, it is glaringly obvious that really effective individuals are the people who recognise that they can—and should—make a commitment to their own personal development. It's easy to become so seduced by new technology—firing off email, trawling the Internet, networking with others via our PCs—that you forget the most important thing of all: *people* need to relate *to people*.

Nothing can take the place of a smile, an understanding ear, a few sentences that indicate you know where the other person is coming from. And now that videoconferencing is becoming more common, technology itself is dictating that you power up your people skills.

As you race to keep up in this Age of Information, you can feel that you must learn something new every day simply to hold your own. However, it's easy to overlook something vitally important that you need to master—the skills of human interaction and communication. Without those, it matters little how well you can find your way around the maze of new technology available to business. If you can't relate to people, you won't have a business to make use of all that new technology.

What is it that draws us to some people more than others? What *is* that 'special something' that those people have? Do they have to work at it? Did they *learn* it somewhere? Were they born with it?

Some people do seem to arrive in this world equipped with sunny personalities and a natural gift for relating to other people. We can all remember people like that from our school days—the lucky ones, who never lacked for friends or interesting things to do.

It would be nice to be born like that, but the truth is that most of us aren't. We amble through life having a success here, making a mistake there, and all the time wishing we could conjure up powerful people skills from somewhere to make life easier.

Well, maybe you have a fairy godmother, but if *I* have, she's never been keen to make my acquaintance! I realised very early in life that no one was ever likely to come along and wave a magic wand and say, 'I've granted your wish, Doug. Here's the kind of personality that will win friends and influence people like never before!'

So I set out to discover what made these people different. I started studying. As well as studying books and listening to tapes, I studied people:

★ what they did
★ how they behaved
★ what they said.

I rapidly understood that many talented people seemed to be able to translate effortlessly their effective communication skills to the podium, and thus influence many others. I went to seminars and lectures, and listened to people who seemed to have little trouble holding the audience in the palms of their hands. How did they do it? What did they say and do that was so different?

Bit by bit, I began to piece it all together. When I did, I realised something very exciting. It *is* possible to work on your people skills. It *is* possible to learn how to attract others. You really *can* mould yourself into the person you would like to be!

You can develop powerful people skills

It's really very simple. Not easy, but simple. Step by step, you can change who you are and what you are. The secret is in controlling the way other people perceive you.

How many times have you wished that your words could convey your thoughts more vividly? How many times have you not been able to express an emotion? How many times have you wished that you could learn the secrets of presenting yourself better—through dress, through words, through actions?

This book will show you how to do just that. You don't have to change your 'inner' self. Your own personality will always come through—it has to. That's what makes you unique. But you can change the way you think about things. You can change the way you view the world and the people in it. You can be more positive, more likeable, and very much in demand. This will have a dramatic effect on both your business success and your social life.

Does it all sound too good to be true?

It isn't, you know.

Powerful people skills are essentially about drawing people to you. But *how* do you do that?

Essentially, by being a good communicator.

You communicate who you are by the way you dress, speak, and act. For example, think of the actors in the last film you saw. Did they have you believing in the characters they played? I bet they did. *How* did they make you believe in them?

★ by projecting themselves into the part

★ by dressing the part

★ by behaving and talking in certain ways.

Take this one step further and think of an actor who has successfully played many different roles. Same person. Same face. Same body. But by changing modes of dress, by speaking different words, by behaving in different ways, they communicate to the audience a totally different character.

If you're not happy with the way other people perceive you, you can change it. But don't think that being a good communicator is solely about changing the surface things. It's a lot more than that. When it comes down to the nitty-gritty, to communicate with others *you have to care about them*. There can be no true communication if you care only about yourself.

Learn from other top communicators

One of the greatest communicators in Australia is a man called John Nevin. John not only founded Salesmen With a Purpose in Australia, but was also the foundation president of the National Speakers Association of Australia. Those who know John would agree with me that his personal achievements are nothing short of outstanding.

What makes him so great?

Without a doubt, it is his skill in and around people. Everybody says the same thing about John: 'What a great communicator!'

He gives. He communicates on *your* terms, not his. It's always 'What have you been doing?'; never 'I've done this' or 'I've done that'. He focuses on you. He listens to you. I still remember the day I first met him. He was more interested in what I was doing than what he had done. I had to find out about his achievements from others.

These days, it's nothing for me to receive a handwritten card from somewhere in the world saying 'Saw this article, thought you might be able to use it', or a simple postcard saying 'How are you?'

Other people—other great communicators—do what John does. Winston Marsh, national speaker and communicator, when he sees items of interest, faxes them to other people. It's called *giving naturally*. It's all about being able and willing to step out of your comfort zone and start communicating.

Susie Elelman is someone else who comes to mind. Susie is a multi-media personality, and her years of media training make her highly responsive when she meets you. She focuses on you immediately, beams a thousand-watt smile and makes you feel that you're the one person in the room she really wants to speak to.

You may think that John Nevin, a professional speaker and management consultant, or Susie, a media personality, are way out of your league. Maybe professionals like them do things differently. Who wants to hear from you?

That's the kind of negative thinking you need to avoid. If you are in a room full of people with similar interests, try communicating by following up. Use the phone, fax or mail. It works for John. It'll work for you. You too can learn magical new ways of communicating. That's what it's all about.

Let's take a closer look at communication.

WHAT IS COMMUNICATION?

How many times have you sat back at some function to listen to a guest speaker and thought enviously, 'I wish I could just get up and speak like that'?

How many times have you watched other people at parties, laughing and chatting easily with others, and wondered what their secret is? Why *is* it that some people can communicate with others as though they were born to it—and others die inside at the very thought of standing on a podium in front of an audience?

First, know that probably at least half of those confident people *are also dying inside*—yes, even while you are watching them! There aren't too many people around who are 'born' with this ability to communicate confidently with others. Most have worked on it. Most have learnt to live with stage fright, with shyness, with uncertainty—in fact, they have learnt how to turn these things to their advantage.

'To their advantage?' you're probably muttering sceptically to yourself right now. 'How can shyness and uncertainty be an *advantage*?'

It's not as silly as it sounds! You'll find that most accomplished speakers feel the same. They've experienced nervousness, clammy palms, even nausea. They know what it feels like to be standing there, fighting the urge to flee in panic, as some big wheel introduces them to an expectant audience. But they have learnt to control those feelings; learnt to use that adrenalin surge as a tool.

You will come to do the same.

There's another side to this, as well. One thing you can be absolutely sure of is that most people's self-esteem is pretty fragile.

You feel shy at that party?

So does every second person.

You feel that your life is dull and boring in comparison with others?

They feel the same about theirs.

You wonder how on earth people carry on such sparkling conversations?

If you were to write down the text of most conversations, you'd find they suddenly seem a lot duller! Communication is about more than words.

Communication is about word power, yes, but it's also about confidence. It's about how you present yourself: your clothes, your hair, your stance. Don't get the wrong idea here. We aren't talking designer clothes and expensive hairdos. We are talking well-cared-for and appropriate.

Communication is about *how you listen*, too. We've all experienced 'conversations' with self-centred people who are positively enchanted with themselves and their own concerns. We've all had our attempts at speech interrupted or met with a token nod before they get back to the *really* interesting subject—themselves. Sound familiar?

Now those kinds of people will eventually find themselves alone at a party. Nobody likes to be talked *at*.

People who can talk easily with others, who can give an entertaining speech or presentation for work, all have one thing in common: *they care about others*. Rather than spending all their energy agonising over what sort of impression they are going to make, their thinking goes something like this:

* 'What are my audience's interests? What do they want to know? How can I help them understand?'
* 'That person over in the corner looks just as shy as I feel. I think I'll go over.'
* 'This girl sure loves her pottery class. I'll see if I can draw her out on it a bit.'
* 'If I really know my subject, it'll be easy to talk about it. I won't have to worry so much about notes.'

The vital first impression

An essential part of communication is *the first impression*. If you *appear* confident, relaxed and knowledgeable, the battle's half over. People get the message, 'This person knows what she's talking about' or 'Hey, this guy's really on my level. I think he'd understand what I'm getting at.'

The initial impression is made before you even open your mouth. Think about it for a moment. If you see a perfect stranger walk into a room or onto a podium, what do you do? You immediately make judgements about the *kind* of person they are according to what they are wearing, how they wear it, how they walk, and their confidence (or lack of it) when they first look at the audience or engage in conversation. You get an overall impression of how they groom themselves. Are they smart or a bit rough around the edges?

Finally, out come the words. You can feel very let down when some well-groomed, interesting-looking person opens their mouth and ruins the good impression they have created by poor speech habits. These can range from a monotonous voice, to poor grammar, to a conversation displaying self-interest or laced with cliches.

Or you have the opposite—a neatly presented but fairly ordinary-looking person starts to talk—and instantly their personality transforms your first impressions. *Wow*, you think. *If only I could use words like that …*

You can. Word power can be learnt.

All communication skills can be learnt—by simply learning a lot more about people.

With the help of this book, you will learn:

★ how your own self-esteem influences the way you communicate with people

★ how to develop confidence

★ how to project a positive personality

★ how to develop your word-power

★ how to improve:
  – the way you look
  – the way you sound
  – what you say
  – how you say it

★ how to listen effectively

★ how to write notes and speeches

★ how to speak effectively with minimal or no notes

★ how to communicate effectively in writing

★ how to put it all together and become a *confident communicator*.

PART 1

BUILDING ON YOUR STRENGTHS

1

BUILDING ON YOUR STRENGTHS

THE CORE OF YOUR PEOPLE SKILLS

You begin to develop your own personal character or identity from the day you are born. The care you were given as an infant and the experiences you have had all through life make you the kind of person you are.

If you look around, you're bound to find that there are some people who have had it better than you, and some who have had it worse. Some people may have been ignored, unloved, abused. Some may come from homes where there was never enough to eat or where six people had to live crammed into three rooms.

Others have had the good fortune to come from secure, loving homes. They have had idyllic childhoods: plenty of nourishing food, plenty of toys and books, a fine education. Then there are those from all the families in between: demonstrative, undemonstrative, one-parent, eccentric, bush-dwellers, city-dwellers, diverse ethnic groups and cultures, and so on.

Against the odds

You don't have to look far before you realise, too, that there are plenty of people who simply delight in making other people's lives miserable.

You will also meet the kind of person who will make you exclaim, 'With all the dreadful things that have happened to him in his life, you wonder how he still can smile!' or 'Isn't it amazing that someone with a background like hers should have made such a success of her life?'

Again and again, you will run across people who have overcome tremendous odds to be who they are and what they are today. You *cannot* use your background as an excuse for being poor, or friendless, or stuck in a dead-end job. 'If only' is not just one of the world's most useless phrases. It's also one of the saddest. Decide now never to use it again.

Let me say now that discussions of psychotherapy or counselling are outside the range of this book. If you think you need these services to change your self-image or self-esteem, by all means consult trained personnel. What I do in this book is explore the world of effective communication.

To communicate effectively you must have some answers to these questions:

* What kind of person am I?
* How do I appear to other people and what influences their behaviour?
* How can I build not only my own self-esteem but that of others to make the job of communicating easier?

Knowing *who you are*, knowing the influences that have made your personality what it is, provides a basis for vastly improved communication skills. So I am operating from *how you present now*.

When you talk about building your people skills you probably mean one or more of the following:

* projecting an image to others that you feel is the real 'you', in the kind of way that will make people like you
* being more interesting to others than you are now
* developing a more powerful personality for the purposes of social and professional success.

In fact, you are really asking these questions:

* What *is* my personality type?
* How *do* other people see me?
* What can I do to improve those aspects of my personality that I don't like?

This book will help you explore those questions. It suggests simple, effective ways to boost your self-confidence so that you can project the kind of personality you want. That personality is actually a part of you right now—just waiting to emerge.

Maybe you're sitting now thinking, 'But if my personality is formed by all these experiences from the time I was born until now, how can I hope to change myself? Is it possible?'

Can you *really* change the way you see and feel about yourself—and the way you relate to others?

Yes. You can.

It takes time, effort and a conscious decision to see it through via a positive action plan. There's a very good reason for the vast numbers of books and articles on the importance of setting goals and using affirmations—*it works!* You've probably heard the old saying, 'If you don't know where you're going, any road will take you there'. This book is all about:

★ making sure you know what your goals are

★ helping you plan to achieve them.

To do it, you will have to take a good long look at the way you view both yourself and other people. You may also have to change some things about the way you act.

Change is from within

Nobody is suggesting that you become a different person. You're still you. All those things that have happened to form you are still there in your past. What you *can* do is take a good long look at them and who you are now. Then you can take steps to overcome the bad influences and maximise the good.

If the change is to be real and lasting, it will mean trying out things for yourself. You have to find out directly from personal experience what works best for you. You will probably find that your identity is made up of a bunch of sub-personalities that emerge at different times, depending on where you are, what you're doing, and who you're with.

Think about your friends, workmates and acquaintances. Some people you won't bother with much. They might think you're quiet, or boring, or grumpy. Others you spend a lot of time with. They might see a different 'you': a smiling, witty person, or someone very efficient, or even the life of the party.

You tend to mirror the behaviour of the person you're with. Importantly, *other people do the same with you.* If you're loud and angry, they'll tend to be the same. If you're happy and smiling, they're likely to smile back. This simple fact greatly influences the impact of your efforts at communication with all sorts of people.

In a nutshell, your personality is the 'you' that other people see. Your *behaviour* may change, depending on who you're with, but your personality remains fairly constant. Your personality is, essentially, the way *you* react to certain cues that is different from the way *other people* react to the same cues. If you don't like the way you typically react, and if you want to change, then you need to look at your self-image and your self-esteem.

YOUR SELF-IMAGE

Your self-image is the picture you have of yourself. You may see yourself as well-dressed, efficient, punctual, hard-working and innovative. Or you may see yourself as an inefficient fat slob. Your view of yourself may be wildly inaccurate or it may be smack on target. Most likely, your view of yourself is correct in some respects but not in others.

Your self-image is largely formed by your *self-esteem*—the value you place on yourself. It is the general opinion you have of yourself, accumulated during and after your childhood—your sense of self-worth.

What many people don't understand is that their belief system, based on their early years, may be *completely wrong*. Any basic psychology textbook will demonstrate how easy it is to 'program' young children and animals.

Suppose, for instance, you were programmed by a mother who had a bad experience with a door-to-door salesman. As a child, you were constantly warned not to open the door to strangers and not to speak to strangers. An obedient child, you did what you were told. As you grew up, this message had burrowed deep into your subconscious: *strangers can't be trusted*.

Now here you are, twenty years down the track. You want a job in sales. Your task is to be a door-to-door salesperson. You can't believe how sick you feel at the prospect. No wonder: *your central nervous system is running amok!* The computer in your brain was programmed one way; now you are trying to change it overnight.

Slow down. Remember, change takes time. You need both practice and lots of feedback from your inner self. Take the time to sit back and examine the possible reasons for your reactions. What negative experiences did you have back in those early days? Some of you will have to think hard. Others (like me) don't have to look very far at all.

School days—the basis of low self-esteem?

My school days were a very negative time for me. I had trouble with every subject. I always tell people in my seminars that I was in the 50 per cent of the class that helped the other 50 per cent get a pass. I can laugh about it now, but it took a long time, and a lot of work and insight, for me to overcome the effect that school had on my self-esteem.

However, I know, from experience, that it can be done.

School was a massive struggle. In hindsight I realise that I was always looking for acceptance and approval. When it wasn't there, I didn't function well. There was no one skill I could master to make me feel better about myself, to allow me to start believing in myself. That came much later in life.

We can't carry the negative influences in our early lives to the grave. We have to deal with them now. At school, I believed I couldn't spell. Forty years later, I *know* I can't spell! The difference is, I can now say light-heartedly, 'If you can spell a word only one way, you are totally inflexible!' (I also know that a very efficient spellcheck is only a matter of a couple of simple commands on the computer.)

It was my low self-image and faulty belief system (that is, 'Since I didn't do well at school, I'll probably never learn') that made it so difficult for me to write my first book. I had a whole lot of knowledge I wanted to communicate to people. I *knew* it was valuable. But I wasn't much of a writer. I couldn't spell. What was I going to do?

I started to read books about writing. I talked to writers. Eventually I enrolled in a four-day workshop on how to write a book. Twenty eager students were there, all waiting for a guru to come and tell us how to write; waiting for the magic words that would make it all possible.

She walked in. She looked around the room and asked, 'How many of you wish to write a book?'

What a silly question, I thought. We had paid a lot of money to be here. Of course we wanted to write a book. All we needed now, sitting there with our pens poised, was for her to impart the secret of how to do it.

Then she told us.

'Just go and write,' she said. 'Write until you bust. Write until you can't write any more. Then edit it. That's the secret of writing a book. You edit and rewrite and edit and then rewrite some more.'

We spent the next three days learning how to do that. For me, the magic was in my change of attitude. I began to think I *could* do it. Here were a series of steps I could follow. Master the steps and it was possible to write a book. My deeply ingrained programming began to change. Instead of telling myself I couldn't possibly do this thing, I began to say to myself, 'I *can* write a book'.

And I did.

I found that this elusive sense of self-worth has a lot to do with *self-talk*—those mental messages we send ourselves all the time.

Self-talk can be positive. It can boost our egos and lead to a positive self-image. Or it can be negative and lead to low self-esteem.

Examples of negative self-talk are:

★ 'I'm never going to be popular.'
★ 'I can't relate to people.'
★ 'I don't know the right things to wear or the right things to say.'
★ 'I'll be out of place.'

Examples of positive self-talk are:

⋆ 'I'm good at drawing people out.'
⋆ 'I look great in this outfit.'
⋆ 'People are always friendly to me.'
⋆ 'I think this speech is going to go well.'

To project a positive image, you need to have a healthy self-image—and that comes about from positive self-talk, plus action!

Unfortunately most people's self-esteem is very easily dented. Everyone goes through rough periods from time to time. You make a few bad judgements, you fail to close an important deal, you have a falling-out with a friend—and suddenly your self-esteem takes a nose-dive.

What happens is that when you go through these periods, you'll find negative thoughts not just nudging at your mind, but battering at the doors! 'I'm no good,' you think to yourself. 'I just haven't got the drive/the talent/the intelligence to do this job/work at this relationship.' Or 'That's not me! I couldn't do that in a million years.'

What's the big danger here?

It's simple! Once you start to lose confidence in yourself and your abilities, your self-esteem takes a corresponding dive—*and you begin to act the part in your daily life*. You *feel* like a loser, so (sometimes unconsciously) you start to *act* like a loser.

The people you meet will pick up the message that you're sending in all sorts of subtle ways. Then they start to *mirror* your attitudes.

What if someone meets you for the first time when you're in this frame of mind? Naturally enough, they'll tend to accept you at your own evaluation. If *you* think you're useless, hopeless, or incompetent, they'll think so too. *You're practically begging people to step on you!*

Let me share with you a story which shows how this 'mirroring' works.

Recently, we were looking for a new staff member. One young person who came in made an immediate impression. Unfortunately, I'm sure it wasn't the one he had hoped to make.

When he came into the room, I looked up with a smile to welcome him. I was met with the usual battery of first impressions that we all receive when we observe someone else for the first time: the way he was dressed (which was okay), his general appearance (neat), his body language (negative) and his speech (*very* negative!).

What did he do wrong?

First, he walked in with a lukewarm smile which was quickly over-shadowed by a frown as we shook hands. Second, his opening words were, 'Will this take long? I've got to catch a train home.'

I'm sure my smile faded as quickly as his. Although we went through the motions for the rest of the interview, he had effectively blown his chances in those first few seconds. His words showed me that he was focusing on what he wanted, rather than on what his prospective employer wanted. So it was quite natural for my attitude to mirror his. He was very effectively telegraphing the message, 'I don't really want to be here'. By choosing someone else for the job, I mirrored back, 'And I don't really want you here!'

His projected image was a reflection of his self-image, which probably arose from self-talk such as:

★ 'People always give me interviews at an inconvenient time.'

or

★ 'I know I'm going to miss the train and I probably won't get the job anyway.'

It was an unsatisfactory interview and a waste of time for both of us.

I am absolutely emphatic about the importance of getting into the habit of positive thinking. Yes, I know, I know! You've heard so much about the power of positive thinking and 'all that claptrap' that you're beginning to tune out.

Don't. There's a reason for people saying those things—over and over and over again—in books and talks and on tapes and on film.

Positive thinking works.

I'm not asking you to be impractical; to live in some fantasy land; to pretend things are great when you've just messed up the best business deal to come your way in the last five years. I don't expect you to perform complicated mental gymnastics in order to ignore situations in your life that make you feel low.

What do I expect?

When I ask you to *stay positive*, I mean:

★ If you make a mistake, look for the good that can come out of it. Learn whatever lesson there is to be learned and put it behind you.

★ Don't place too much importance on a mistake-free existence. *Mistakes are part of life*.

★ Keep your thoughts and your words positive. Don't be a knocker. Don't hold grudges. Remember, negative feelings and opinions create a negative atmosphere—which is definitely not conducive to good communication!

You will find that if you try—*really* try—to follow these rules, other people will begin to treat you differently and your self-esteem will, in turn, begin to rise as if by magic. Things get better. You will begin to develop more powerful skills in relating to and communicating with others.

Don't you feel more attracted to happy, confident people?

Don't you feel more like doing business with them?

Don't you find it much, much easier to communicate with them?

A couple of years ago, I served on the executive committee of an organisation which had been formed to help people develop self-confidence, self-esteem and communication skills. Things went well for a while. Then, for one reason or another, several key people were no longer able to serve on the committee. One had a genuine reason, but a couple of others were simply 'too busy'. It's the kind of problem that besets most committees from time to time. We could have ridden out the problem—except for one person, whom I'll call Joanne.

Joanne came to every meeting. She was hard-working. She was organised. She was dedicated to the aims of the organisation—*in theory*. In reality, her own self-esteem was so low that there was little hope of her bolstering the self-esteem of anyone else. She was one of the most negative people I have ever met in my life.

From the moment she walked into the room, I could feel my shoulders begin to tense. It got to the stage where I would sit, teeth on edge, waiting for her first complaint.

If it wasn't the extra paperwork caused by so-and-so not sending in a report on time, it was the fact that nobody really appreciated the amount of work she put in. Or the membership lists needed updating. The agenda had the wrong priorities. And so on and so on and so on …

We were all only too well aware of the effect this person was having on the rest of us. We tried offering help. (*No, she preferred to do it herself so she'd know it was done properly.*) We pointed out the good things that were happening. (*Yes, but it would have been so much better if ...*)

Finally things came to a head when another valued committee member blew his stack.

'Joanne, I've got better things to do than come here every week and listen to this,' he said tightly, halfway through the meeting. 'According to you, nothing's ever right. Nobody else's suggestions are worth anything. You'll only ever be happy on a committee of one!'

Eventually Joanne resigned. The committee recovered, filled the vacant positions, planned a dynamic new program and surged ahead. One negative person had soured the whole experience. It really was a case of everyone she met being her mirror—the only trouble was, the whole group was in danger of catching her negativity!

Don't let something like this happen to you. If you let the negative thinkers suck you in, you'll become one of them in no time. Look for positive friends and colleagues. They're out there—in great numbers.

How do you find them?

Simple. You send out the *positive vibes* that you want to see reflected in others' faces.

The negative thinkers will be repelled. Like Joanne, those who want to wallow in their own gloom will eventually slink off and find others who want to wallow along with them.

Avoid the wallowers—and build up your own self-esteem in the process!

Now we have the basics in place, let's take a look at your action plan. You've made the decision to change. Now it's time to make sure you reach your goals by planning your strategy.

YOUR ACTION PLAN

1 Affirmation

Write a description (or affirmation) of the New You. For example:

I am slim and healthy, and radiate self-confidence. I can talk to individuals, groups or large gatherings with ease. I speak fluently, and always know enough about my subject to hold people's interest. I have a genuine interest in and empathy with others. I am not overawed by those who are more powerful or famous than I am, because I know I am an interesting person ... etc.

_____

_____

_____

_____

_____

_____

_____

2   Goals

Write down the things you think you need to work on. Choose one area to work on at a time, and write down the short-term and mid-term goals you will need to achieve on your way to the New You.

Area of need	Goal
a	
b	
c	
d	

3   Action to achieve goals

Make a list of the things you will need to do in order to achieve each of your goals.

Goal:

To do:

_____

_____

_____

4 Achievements

As you reach each goal, write down:

* ★ how you achieved it, and
* ★ how you feel it has affected:
    * **a** your self-image
    * **b** your projected image.

By doing this, you'll be able to look back over your progress at any time and see how far you've come. Success breeds success! Every triumph, no matter how small, gives you increased confidence to tackle the next step.

> **Goal:**
> _____
> **Achieved:**
> _____
> **Effect on self-image:**
> _____
> **Effect on projected image:**
> _____

5 Evaluation and future directions

Sometimes your goals will change. You might find the New You wanting to go off in a direction you hadn't expected.

That's fine. Life is, after all, a never-ending learning experience. It makes sense, after reaching each milestone, to re-evaluate your goals. Are they still the same? If they no longer seem relevant, set new ones.

Even if you stay on the path you planned and reach the main goal you set for your new personality, it's not an excuse for standing still and growing cobwebs. If you're not growing, you're decaying. Never, never stop learning!

> **Goals achieved:**
> _____
> **New challenges:**
> _____

2

HOW TO BUILD A POSITIVE SELF-IMAGE

It's fine to talk about thinking positively and staying away from negative people. But you're probably wishing someone could wave a magic wand and give you a positive self-image right *now*. How are you supposed to project a positive self-image to others when you feel lower than a flat-bellied snake?

Well, assuming you're ready at least to *start* thinking positively, let's look at a few down-to-earth ways of improving things for you *today*.

Here are two suggestions:

★ Become an actor.
★ Identify the areas you need to work on, and work on one at a time.

BECOME AN ACTOR

Now, you *can* run out and join an amateur theatre group if you want to. Maybe that's a secret desire you've always had. Most of us, however, haven't got the time or inclination to do that.

More practical is to adopt the role of an actor in your everyday life. It's not as difficult as you might first think. In fact, it can be downright fun. Furthermore, this idea of *acting* like the person you want to be in order to *become* the person you want to be has its basis in plenty of psychological studies. Start acting like a confident, positive person, and you will find a certain kind of magic takes place. You will actually begin to *feel* positive.

Why does this happen?

People treat you according to the way they see you

Part of the reason you begin to feel positive is that people start treating you according to the way they see you. Think about it—don't you

do exactly the same thing? It's natural to form opinions about people according to how they speak or behave. If you encounter a person who acts with authority, you tend to treat them with a certain amount of respect (or caution!): 'This person sounds as if she knows what she's talking about', '*This guy sounds like he's in charge*'.

Imagine that you were interviewing prospective employees for a receptionist's position. Would you employ someone who was slightly grubby, carelessly dressed and poorly-spoken for the position? Or would you employ the candidate who was neatly dressed, articulate and made lots of eye contact with you?

You treat people according to their projected image. Logically, you must expect other people to do the same to you.

But how do you go about projecting a confident image to others when you're uncertain, shy or afraid? How can you act a part or play out a role?

One way is to emulate someone you know and admire; someone who relates to others exactly as you would like to. Naturally there are some limits—you can't manufacture instant beauty or an ability with witty repartee. However, you *can* make the most of the looks you have or cultivate a ready smile.

Personality is more than physical appearance or the ability to crack jokes, of course. Carefully watch the other ways in which your 'model' relates to people. Do they listen to others? What do they talk about? Do they make eye contact? How do they sit, and stand? How do they dress?

Observe more than one person. Pick out the things that they do that would comfortably merge with your own personality. Then practise those habits or mannerisms one at a time. A word of caution here. Don't imitate personal little quirks that may be attractive or cute on your model, but look contrived or even irritating if *you* copy them. Remember, you're looking for their manner, not their *mannerisms*.

Practise your new 'personality' on strangers. (No, I don't mean pick up strangers in a bar or off the street—there are some weird people out there!) By 'strangers' I mean people you meet at seminars, business meetings, parent groups, professional associations, hobby courses, the gym—people who don't know you (yet) or don't know you very well. This gives you a chance to try out new ways of dealing with people without risking hearing someone mutter in the background, 'What's with Jack today? Something's up, he's not acting like himself at all'.

Acting the part of the kind of person you want to be will go a long way towards getting you there. But always *act in keeping with your own personality*. And how will you know what suits your personality? You'll feel comfortable in that particular role.

As you can see, you *can* build up the kind of image you want to project. But if all you're ever doing is playing a part, you may have the constant fear that one day your house of cards is going to come toppling down all around you. You fear that one day, people will find out who you *really* are ... and what then?

Obviously, the solution is to blend your *desired image* (how you want others to see you) with your *self-image* (how you see yourself). You need to feel so comfortable with your projected image that it becomes a second skin, not a disguise.

If you want to work on your self-image, it follows that you are not satisfied with it. Inevitably this is because you feel that you are *lacking* in something; you're not happy with who you are. And if you're not happy with who you are, then you are suffering from low *self-esteem*. You don't like yourself; you want to be different—in short, you want to be someone else.

FIND THE AREAS YOU NEED TO WORK ON

How much you value yourself as a person is influenced by:

★ how you believe others see you
★ how much others appear to value you.

But just how *do* you think others see you? This can be difficult to assess. After all, we tend to have a distorted view of our own personalities. You could ask friends, but they'll often tone it down because they don't want to hurt your feelings. You could ask someone who *doesn't* like you, but that response will probably be biased too!

You can get some idea of your level of self-esteem by writing about yourself from the point of view of several different people: close friends, acquaintances, your parents, your children. Pretend that each of these people is writing a letter to someone else to tell them about you.

What do you think would be the key points they would make about you as a person? What would they praise? What would they condemn?

You'll probably find that the letters would have some things in common. However, one or two of the letters would mention things that reflect a facet of your personality shown only to certain people. This is to be expected: we are different things to different people.

This is how two letters might describe someone ('John') in quite different ways.

Letter written by John from the point of view of his boss:

> *John works very hard for the company. He is always punctual and prepared to work longer hours if necessary to get the job done. He is efficient and organised, can work to a deadline, and relates well to other members of staff. He inspires other staff members to give of their best.*

Letter written by John from the point of view of his wife:

> *I know John works hard and is well-thought of at work, but I wish he spent a bit more time with his family. The trouble is he's too much of a perfectionist—and he expects the rest of us to have the same standards as he has. Everything has to be the best: the best organised, the best presented, on time or, better still, ahead of time. He's a workaholic, so he's too tired to talk much when he gets home. He doesn't seem to have any interests apart from his job …*

Now, sit right down and write yourself some letters!

After you have finished this exercise, write down how you feel about being described in this way. Do you like the person they have written about? If not, how do you want to change?

Your reactions are the key to your self-esteem. If you can take in what your 'friends' have written and accept the good with the bad, you've probably got a fairly healthy level of self-esteem. But if the descriptions seem to be full of faults and inadequacies, it's likely that your sense of self-esteem has been undermined and you've a somewhat negative view of yourself as a person. If you are *not* happy to be the person described, then you have some work in front of you.

3

WORKING ON YOUR SELF-ESTEEM

To begin improving your self-image, you probably need to raise the level of your self-esteem. Think about that 'self-image' you just described in the previous section.

How do you feel about yourself?

What do you see to be your good and bad points?

Make two lists:

1   your good points—your virtues and your strengths
2   your negative points—your vices and your weaknesses.

When writing out your lists, take these aspects into account:

★   your appearance
★   your attitude to work
★   your home life
★   your relationships
★   your personal manner.

These lists will give you useful feedback about your level of self-esteem. Which list is the longest? If it's list 2, your self-esteem needs a boost. If it's list 1, your self-esteem is fairly healthy and you may have just one or two areas to work on to make you feel better about yourself.

The first thing you should do is go back over the list of negatives and see where you are obviously putting yourself down. Look for words like 'too vague' or 'stupid' or 'procrastinate all the time'. *Cross them out* and replace them with more specific and less emotive words. For example, 'stupid' could be 'need more information', 'procrastinate all the time' could be 'need to decide priorities'.

Notice how most of those negative terms serve only to attack your ego rather than the problem. Labels like 'I'm lazy', for instance, are deadly. They virtually paralyse you. (How can you change laziness? You're too lazy to try, right?)

Take a closer look at a label like that. I bet you're not lazy in every aspect of your life. Give you something to accomplish in an area where you have a vital interest, and it's probably a case of full steam ahead.

Dig deeper. When you say, 'I'm lazy', ask yourself, 'in relation to what?' Here are a few examples of where 'I'm lazy' means other things entirely.

'I'm lazy.'
In relation to what?
'Getting out of this dead-end job. I hate it, but I'm too lazy to find anything different.'

In this case, 'lazy' could equal:

★ fear
★ lack of confidence
★ unwillingness to take risks because of financial responsibilities.

'I'm lazy.'
In relation to what?
'Getting this project under way.'

In this case, 'lazy' could equal:

★ 'I don't know where to start.' (lack of direction, lack of information)
★ 'The job's too big.' (fear)
★ 'I don't have enough experience.' (fear, lack of information or guidance)

'I'm lazy.'
In relation to what?
'I'm so disorganised with washing, ironing, cleaning.'

In this case, 'lazy' could equal:

★ 'I've got too much to do, and not enough help.'
★ 'I'm working two jobs: at home and at work.'
★ 'I don't have enough time to do everything.'
★ 'I need to know more about time management.'

Just as you have to read between the lines to know what *other* people really mean, you sometimes have to do it with yourself! We're all too ready to put ourselves down, instead of analysing the real reasons for lack of self-esteem.

If you have thought that laziness is one of your weaknesses, when you look at these changes, you should feel better already! You have given yourself something concrete to work on. You'll feel a great deal better about yourself, a great deal more in control, when you decide on the areas you need to work on. Feel certain that you *can* change—*and the first step is to change your opinion about yourself.*

BUILDING SELF-CONFIDENCE

It's reassuring to know that building your self-esteem automatically means that you'll be building self-confidence at the same time. And, happily, self-confidence makes communicating with others a breeze!

If you feel good about yourself, if you value your abilities, then you will see the effects of this improved self-esteem in a confident, assertive attitude towards other people.

However, don't make the mistake of thinking that being positive and assertive means that you can hog the limelight. People who lack self-confidence tend to talk about themselves and their own interests all the time. With your new-found positive outlook, you have no need to do that. There's nothing guaranteed to bring communication to a halt more quickly!

At a recent seminar, I glanced around the room and caught the eye of Alison, a woman I see in meetings from time to time. She waved, said something to the person she was talking to and threaded her way across the room towards me.

'Hi, Alison,' I said. 'How have you been?'

'Busy, busy. You know how it is.' She glanced back over her shoulder to the woman she had just left. 'Thank goodness you came in just then. I was desperate for an opportunity to get away from that woman! Who is she? Have you seen her before?'

'Jan,' I nodded. 'Bit overpowering, was she?'

She rolled her eyes. 'What an experience! At first I thought she was great, really entertaining. But she's absolutely exhausting. I've been talking to her for fifteen minutes, and I don't think I've got in more than two words.'

'She's always like that,' I said. 'A little bit goes a long way.'

We've all met the type, haven't we? They may be witty, articulate, born entertainers. But they can't bear anyone else having the floor. They like people to sit at their feet and look adoringly at them. A little bit does indeed go a long way. After a while, we want to turn off, to crawl away, to hide—*because there's no communication.*

No matter how much self-confidence you have, it is essential that you understand and relate to others. Otherwise you'll find that sense of emptiness returning before too long, and your self-esteem will begin to erode again.

UNDERSTANDING AND RELATING TO OTHERS

It's hard enough to figure out just who we are and learn how to project a positive image. But we've also got to figure out what makes other people tick! People are all so different. We like some, we don't like others. What makes people behave the way they do? How can we relate well to people? Is there a set of rules somewhere to help?

No. There's no set of rules. But there *are* a few simple *understandings* about people which will help you enormously. Learn a few simple skills in dealing with people, and you will automatically improve your own success and confidence.

You have learnt something about improving your own self-esteem. You know how easily your opinion of yourself can be dented. You know how one grumpy person or one critical comment can make you feel bad for the rest of the day. Worse, it can have a snowball effect so that *you* take out your hurt on other people so *they* have a bad day too! All of these insights into how *your* mind works will help you in understanding how other people's minds work, too. We're all surprisingly alike, really.

Here is a list of things to help you understand why others behave as they do. You may find some explanations for some of your own behaviour as well:

★ Early childhood influences tend to influence adult behaviour.

★ We are all more interested in ourselves than anything else.

★ We communicate as much through our bodies as through words.

★ Satisfy the other person's need for self-esteem and he or she becomes more friendly and approachable.

★ We can't help the way we feel, but we *can* help the way we react.

★ Help others like themselves better and we will find them easier to get along with.

★ We often blame other people for what we do not like in ourselves.

★ Labels that people attach to us limit our freedom and our potential for achievement.

★ When we remind ourselves that other people *are* important, our attitude will communicate itself to other people.

★ Our own attitudes are reflected back to us from other people.

★ Act enthusiastically, and we arouse the enthusiasm of others; act confidently and others will have confidence in us.

★ Other people tend to accept us at our own evaluation.

★ We need to realise that other people are different and that this is reasonable and logical.

★ Conflict is basic to life; it comes with growth.

THE POWER OF CHOICE

One of the biggest factors in having a positive self-image is the amount of *choice* we feel we have in life. It's pretty hard to be positive if we constantly have the feeling that our lives are dictated by other people or by fate. We all like to feel that we have some sort of say over the direction our lives will take.

So, once you have isolated the things that contribute to any feelings of low self-esteem (and taken a good look at them to see what they *really* mean) look at your choices in life.

Sure, you know you want to change. You want to become more outgoing. You want people to like you. You want to make some sort of contribution that will be noticed. But it's a bit hard to do any of that if you don't have a sense of control.

The feeling of having 'no choice' prevents us from doing so much. *Note:* I did not say the *fact* of having no choice. I said the *feeling*. There's a big difference because, ultimately, we *do* have a choice.

Don't like your job?

You can choose to:

1   stay
    for the security/prestige/to avoid scenes at home if you quit
2   leave
    to try something you like better/to study/to have a rest
3   stay, but get further qualifications
    to help you obtain the job you really want
4   stay, but take a second job
    to build up a nest egg so you can leave later/to get experience in
    another area
5   stay, but set yourself a deadline to leave
    set a deadline of six months, twelve months, two years or whatever
    and stick to it.

You see? You weigh up the alternatives, you give the pros and cons a rating, and *you make a choice.*

A word about training

You must be completely honest with yourself while you're examining your options in the workplace. Are your feelings about your job coloured by the fact that you lack certain skills? Or perhaps you've been passed over for someone with superior qualifications?

Take a moment to think about your attitude and your skills from your employer's point of view. Employers like people who are *self-directed*. They hire and promote those who have shown an eagerness to better themselves, via part-time work, study, courses, or skill in making and maintaining contacts. They know it's unlikely that talent will be found in someone who is always sitting around waiting for other people to provide them with things.

You can prevent yourself from becoming obsolete. The key to marketing yourself in the new millennium lies in one word: *flexibility*.

Ask yourself these five questions:

1   Did you do at least 32 hours of training related to your own industry in the last 12 months?
2   How many books did you read in the last year:
    a in your own skills area?
    b to broaden your general knowledge?
3   What new skill did you develop in the last 12 months?
4   What new acquaintances have you met who stimulate you to think and achieve?
5   What new goals did you set, and which areas did you target for personal improvement in the last 12 months?

Never be tempted to sit back complacently and feel safe in your job, simply because you perform it competently. Today, you need more. Things have changed. Once, people were happy to care for the delicate stylus on their phonogram, and work at keeping their records scratch-free—until laser beams and CDs changed their perception of what was acceptable. In the same way that people now expect more of the goods they buy, employers expect more of employees.

The information age is upon us, and with the explosion of knowledge it is essential that you show that *you* are an 'upgradable facility'. That way, employers need not fear that they will be 'buying' a product with built-in obsolescence. There are no excuses. You have a wide choice of methods to upgrade your skills: through films, videos, audiotapes, books, meetings, seminars, and clubs of all kinds—not to mention a smorgasbord of challenging educational courses and the Internet.

If you haven't done anything yet, start now. Look upon ongoing learning as a welcome adventure, not an imposition. The time you invest in extra courses, training, or self-improvement will do wonders to boost your self-esteem. And could completely change your attitude to your job.

However, leaving the issue of training aside, suppose you really can't take the stress of a hated job another minute. You could throw yourself under a train (that'll show 'em!), or you could develop a psychosomatic illness so that you 'can't' work. Or you could sit down, weigh up the alternatives and *make a decision*. Be in charge. Perhaps, after making lists, you have to acknowledge that leaving your job may mean any one (or more) of the following:

★   marital disharmony
★   selling the house

★ reduced living standards

★ looking forward to getting up in the mornings.

Is it worth it?

If you decide to stay, at least it has been your choice. If you decide to leave, it has been your choice. *You are in charge of your own destiny.*

Going through this process will make an incredible difference to your self-image. Try writing down all the possible courses of action you could take in any area where you feel you have 'no choice'. Be creative! Then write down the pros and cons of each one. Ask:

★ What is the worst thing that could happen?

★ What is the best thing that could happen?

★ What is *most likely* to happen?

Now make your choice. *You* have made it, nobody else. Set a time a few months hence to review your decision. And if you feel it's turned out to be the wrong one, list your choices *again*. What are your options *now*?

At any given moment in time, the road ahead of you will have several branches, each offering a different opportunity or outcome. Exciting, isn't it? Ask yourself, 'Is this the real me living this life? Or someone I don't even feel I know very well—someone made up by family, friends and workmates?'

Look for the real you. Decide what you want, then tailor your life to get it. Get to know yourself!

TEST YOURSELF

I mentioned earlier that employers look for people who are self-directed when they are employing or promoting staff. At this stage, while you are trying to work out your strengths and weaknesses, it would be a good idea to work your way through the following quiz. It will give you some idea of your degree of *self-direction, inner determination*, and *ability to establish rapport*.

The quiz consists of twenty pairs of statements. Choose the one of each pair that most consistently applies to you and mark it with a cross. If *both* statements apply, put an 'X' beside the one that applies *most*, even if the difference is not very great.

Don't try to give the 'right' answer, because there isn't one! Give the answer that is *true for you*. After all, nobody else is going to see the results. And we all know there's no point in trying to fool ourselves!

Please don't look at the answer key until you have finished the quiz.

Quiz

1   **a** I know where I am heading in life.
      b I am prepared to follow whims and opportunities.

2   **a** I find myself becoming bored with things.
      b I am rarely or never bored.

3   **a** Meeting the standards and expectations of my fellow workers and clients is most important.
      b Meeting my own standards and expectations is most important.

4   **a** I sometimes doubt that I'll 'measure up' for a particular demand.
      b I never doubt my ability to handle a challenge.

5   **a** Handling a crisis brings out the best in me.
      b I'd rather hand over a crisis to the best qualified person.

6   **a** I am rarely anxious about the prospect of failure.
      b I often have twinges of anxiety about failure.

7   **a** The approval of other people is important to me.
      b My own satisfaction with myself is important to me.

8   **a** I never put myself down.
      b I find that I can forestall or reduce criticism from others by blaming myself.

9   **a** I am so busy and have so many jobs and tasks that some may never be finished.
      b I make sure that important tasks are completed as required.

10   **a** I feel that I am using my talents and abilities very effectively.
      b I have many unused talents and abilities.

11   **a** I have yet to accomplish the things I most want to do.
      b I am accomplishing the things I most want.

12   **a** Personal relationships do not mean all that much to me.
      b I am very satisfied with my interpersonal relationships.

13   **a** I believe that two people can get along best if each feels free to express their feelings.
      b I believe that people can generally get on better if they keep their feelings to themselves.

14   **a** I can usually organise my time to fit my activities.
      b I am often frustrated by lack of time.

15   **a** I suffer from indecision more often than I'd like to.
      b I never or rarely suffer from indecision.

16   **a** I can give to others without needing appreciation in return.
      b I dislike giving unless I get some appreciation or other return.

17   **a** I really need to make my own mistakes in order to learn.
      b I can learn from other people's mistakes.

18   **a** I get anxious if I know I'll be late for an appointment.
      b I try always to be punctual, but lateness doesn't make me anxious.

19   **a** I feel free to be myself and bear the consequences.
      b I like to be fairly guarded and avoid embarrassing myself or others.

20   **a** Despite my best efforts, sometimes my feelings are hurt.
      b If I manage situations well, I can always avoid being hurt.

Key

What the quiz reveals about your self-direction, inner determination, and ability to establish rapport with others:

1   **a** has clear aims
     b needs to set goals in order to seize opportunities that are consistent with goals

2   **a** needs to set challenging goals
     b avoids boredom—self-sufficient

3   **a** may prefer to follow rather than lead
     b is not bound by convention

4   **a** may lose opportunities through self-doubt
     b has no fear of inadequacy

5   **a** is self-reliant—especially in a crisis
     b is more of a team player than a leader

6   **a** is self-confident—has no fear of failure
     b frequent self-doubt shows little inner direction

7   **a** is disinclined to act without support
     b does not need the approval of others

8   **a** does not self-belittle
     b lacks confidence in own abilities

9 a finds it difficult to delegate or be assertive
   b is able to complete tasks, schedule times

10 a makes use of talents and abilities
    b needs to work at being self-directed in order to use talents

11 a the lack of a sense of achievement could affect progress
    b makes satisfying achievements

12 a ability to establish rapport could be affected by lack of quality personal relationships
    b has good quality personal relationships

13 a feels free to express feelings
    b is undemonstrative—may seem 'guarded' to others

14 a manages time well
    b needs to develop time-management strategies

15 a has an indecisive attitude that may impede progress
    b is decisive

16 a has the ability to give freely of self
    b risks being seen as self-centred or uncooperative

17 a is a hands-on person who learns best from experience
    b has the ability to learn from others

18 a may be bound by convention—needs to develop strategies for coping with the unexpected
    b displays freedom from convention-bound anxiety

19 a shows acceptance of and confidence in self
    b needs to develop more self-confidence

20 a shows acceptance of own sensitivity
    b efforts to avoid pain may impede progress

The above quiz is designed to give you some degree of insight into your own preferences, traits and habits, and the degree to which they support your efforts to project the image you want. If you examine your answers closely, you are likely to find that certain responses group together.

For instance, *1, 2, 3* and *7* tell you about the extent of your self-direction. If you answered *1a, 2b, 3b* and *7b*, you are a person who has clear aims, you are self-sufficient, you are not bound by convention, and you do not feel you need the approval of others to pursue your goals. In other words, you show a high degree of self-direction.

If, on the other hand, you answered *1b, 2a, 3a* and *7a*, it seems that you could progress faster if you set more challenging goals, and that you should be alert for opportunities that will take you towards these goals. You may find, too, that you prefer to be a follower rather than a leader. There's nothing wrong with that, if you feel happiest working that way. Not everyone wants to be a leader. The most important things for you to know are:

1 what you want
2 how you can get it.

Your answers to this quiz should help you to clarify the best way for you to achieve your goals, and reveal areas in which you may be lacking confidence. Keep in mind always that you will bloom under conditions that suit *you*, not some Superman or Wonder Woman.

The following responses have been grouped for your convenience:

Answers which indicate that you prefer to be a team player or a follower rather than a leader: *3a, 5b, 7a, 9a, 10b, 14b, 15a*

Answers which indicate that you need to work on boosting your self-confidence: *4a, 6b, 7a, 8b, 15a, 16b, 18a, 19b*

Answers which indicate that you find it easy to establish rapport with others: *12b, 13a, 16a*

Answers which indicate that you have a firm understanding of where you're going in life: *1a, 2b, 10a, 11b, 15b*

PART II

PROJECTING A POSITIVE SELF-IMAGE

4

HOW PEOPLE JUDGE YOU

THAT VITAL FIRST IMPRESSION

To know how people make assessments about you, think about how *you* judge others. Suppose you've just laid eyes on someone for the first time. What do you notice first?

Generally, you notice the obvious things: the colour of their skin, whether they're male or female, their approximate age and their general appearance. Of course, if someone's dressed like a complete slob, that may be the first thing you notice, but generally it's much as I've listed.

Only after noticing the major physical characteristics do you start to notice things like facial expressions, eye contact, movement, personal space and so on.

Have you noticed that so far I haven't even mentioned 'what people sound like'? That's because (unless a raucous voice or melodious tones calls our attention to the person in the first place) we judge others initially by what we *see*. Then we confirm or adjust those impressions once we get to know them better.

Always remember: there's no second chance at a first impression!

If you make a bad first impression, it can be well-nigh impossible to get people to change their minds about you. On the other hand, I'm sure you've heard someone say in surprise, 'And I thought he was such a *nice* person when I first met him!' when someone else acted in a way that upset their first impressions.

Rightly or wrongly, people tend to trust their first impressions. Naturally, therefore, you want to make the best first impression that you can. Later on we'll look at speech and effective speaking in all kinds of situations.

But *first*, you need to get your appearance right.

Does this sound as if I want to make you all into clones, like Ira Levin's *Stepford Wives*? Relax. That's not part of becoming 'really you'.

No, what you need to do is to make the most of what you have. And that means looking after your health as carefully as you would an expensive car or a rare flower. It means dressing for success—*your* version of success. It means, in short, letting everything about you 'say' to people exactly what you want them to hear.

What if you have a feature that you hate but really can't hide? A big nose or protuberant eyes? Or what if you're short and weedy-looking instead of statuesque with a commanding presence? And what about things like your gender or ethnic group? You can't change those things.

I repeat: *make the most of what you have*. There's absolutely no point wishing you were taller or worrying because you have a weak chin. No matter what you look like, if you walk into a room with confidence, people notice. Your general bearing is part of that first impression. A pleasant smile and eye contact make a difference too.

Many powerful communicators are not impressive at first glance, but as soon as they start to speak listeners fall under their spell. Every one of us knows someone who fits into this category: friends or co-workers who look very ordinary, but who always win people over with their personalities and communication skills. Don't focus on what you perceive to be negative aspects of your appearance. Concentrate on warmth and rapport—in other words, a genuine interest in the other person.

Studies have shown that non-verbal communication can account for more than half of the 'message' you convey. By paying attention to your total appearance (clothes, grooming, posture, facial expression, gestures, way of walking) you can influence people to form the kind of opinions about you that you want, even before you've opened your mouth.

Let's look at each component of your appearance.

POSTURE AND GESTURES

Why is it that when we are meeting someone for the first time, or walk up onto a stage in front of a crowd of people, we sometimes become super-conscious of our bodies? It's almost like peering out of some lumbering machine. How do I walk naturally? What do I do with my hands? How do I hold my head?

Often we end up looking at our feet in embarrassment, which almost automatically means that our shoulders slump. Or we walk like some jerking robot, our arms swinging unnaturally, our body pitched forward. All of which usually creates quite the opposite of the impression we'd hoped for!

The best advice is to look straight at the person you're approaching, smiling as though you're greeting a well-liked friend. A brief glance to either side is fine to break the intensity—but *don't* gaze at the floor as if you're expecting it to be salted with landmines. (Do, of course, glance around enough so that you're not tripping over steps, electrical cords or people!) Practise walking with confidence and energy.

Confidence is the key. It doesn't matter what size you are: if you relax, everything will be fine.

Whether you're sitting or standing, *an upright posture conveys an impression of alertness, interest and power*. Don't confuse *upright* with *ramrod*, unless you want to look as though you stepped straight from an army graduation parade. A basic upright posture also gives you the leeway, in a discussion, to lean forward a little (a sign of interest and attention) or back (a signal that you're unconvinced, annoyed, bored or relaxed).

Gestures can tell people a lot about you, so it's worthwhile practising a few in front of a mirror. That'll help you eliminate the vague hand-flutter that leaves people concentrating more on whether you're going to knock over their drinks than on what you're saying. Try to cultivate the habit of gesturing *naturally* to illustrate what you're saying or to convey a message: holding up your palm in a 'stop' gesture, or both palms turned up to indicate 'well, that's my proposal!' or 'so what could I do?' Such gestures are natural because humans have been practising them for thousands of years. They are an essential communication tool whenever humans meet.

Keep your hands away from your face (hands at the face tend to indicate insecurity or lying); and of course don't wipe your nose or clean out your ears! Off-putting fixed smiles or strained expressions tend to appear when people tune out. If you really *listen* to what the other person is saying, appropriate facial expressions will come naturally from what you're hearing. Your face will mirror interest, sympathy and so on.

The only thing you might have to guard against (if you don't want the speaker to know what you're really thinking) is an involuntary expression of distaste if you don't like what you hear. Nodding to indicate you're paying attention is fine, within limits (you don't want to look like a human metronome), but be careful that an unwary nod doesn't signal agreement when you *don't* agree.

In short: sit upright, stand upright, make effective gestures, look confident.

GROOMING

People think better of you if you're well-groomed, whether you're male or female, and whatever your personality. By all means keep your individuality, but if you're going to a function and you're not sure of what 'look' to aim for, the rules are pretty simple.

Strive always to look neat and well groomed, and go for the middle ground. Your hair should be well cut in a style that suits you. Avoid extremes of hairstyle and colouring (unless, of course, flamboyance is the impression you *want* to create). For women, make-up should suit your colouring, be expertly applied and not look overdone. If you chew your nails, try to lick the habit (no pun intended!). Short, clean, well-kept nails are okay; ragged and/or grubby nails are not. If you use nail polish, make sure it's not chipped or growing out and that the colour is conservative.

CLOTHES

The saying 'clothes make the man' has been around a long, long time—and it's right on the money. H. D. Thoreau gave us food for thought when he said: 'It is an interesting question how far men would retain their relative rank if they were divested of their clothes.'

The minute you walk into a room, what you are wearing contributes to the way you are judged. I don't mean that people are pointing and whispering and making snide comments (although they might be, if you're wearing something totally inappropriate). I mean that in the little computer that works non-stop in everyone's brain, messages are being sent to the clearing centre—*about you*. A few lightning fast flashes, and the information stored in the computer could look something like this:

… Female … Early thirties. Confident. Nice suit. Nice shoes. Hmmm, looks interesting …

Or, less agreeably:

Female … Looks a bit grim. Got out of the wrong side of the bed maybe? Suit needs a press … who else is here?

Same person. Totally different impression, depending on whether you've taken time and trouble with your appearance. These kinds of judgements are made every day in countless situations, from offices to boardrooms to playgroups. They're made whether you work full-time, part-time or not at all; whether you work inside the home or outside; whether you're male or female. Of course, the whole process is usually subconscious. You're not likely to put your impressions into words.

Years ago, I used to go into any clothing shop and always buy clothes of the same colour—blue. Subconsciously, I was saying, 'I feel good in blue'. Every time I bought a new suit I would happily add it to the blue line-up in my wardrobe.

Then I encountered young Johnny, a dynamic store salesman. Before long he had coaxed me out of my blue comfort zone and into the risky world of other colours. Whenever he saw me looking at blue suits, he'd come up with something else over his arm as an alternative.

'I wouldn't wear that!' I'd protest.

'All the more reason why you should!' he'd respond firmly.

Gradually Johnny helped me to make changes in my life—and I'm glad I had the sense to listen to a professional who knew what he was doing. It's always a good idea to take advice from people who are experts in their field.

Let the professionals help you with changing your image. If you feel anxious listening to them, it's a sign that you are being pushed out of your comfort zone, as I was. As I *had* to be.

Johnny didn't leave it at changing colours, either. He introduced me to new styles as well—what he jokingly referred to as 'today' clothes. Every so often he'd phone and say, 'I've got some "today" clothes for you!' Off I'd go to his shop, to find that he'd made up extra labels and attached them to the shirts, trousers, or suits. The labels said, 'TODAY' CLOTHES.

With a grin, Johnny would bring them out and announce, 'This is today—you've got to wear them!'

If you want to see how close you've stuck to your comfort zone, go and take a look at your wardrobe to see if everything's a similar colour, shape or style.

Keep in mind that your overall look and style start 'selling' you to other people before they know anything else about you. Next time you are in a room full of people, see who stands out because of their general style and presentation. You'll learn a lot.

Even when you're pushing a shopping trolley around the supermarket, other people will categorise you by your dress and grooming. (Why else do we hope we won't meet anyone we know when we dash to the mall on a Saturday afternoon in gardening shorts and a grubby T-shirt to buy a hose nozzle?)

If people aren't quickly attracted to you (or even worse, *don't like* what they see and hear in that first two or three minutes) you'll be dismissed as being unimportant, irrelevant, or even someone to avoid.

Here are some tips to help you make sure that doesn't happen:

1   **Dress for the occasion**
    If you turn up for dinner in a printed shirt and jeans when everyone else is in a suit, you're likely to feel uncomfortable all night. Not only will people make judgements about you according to how you look, but you'll probably worry so much about looking out of place that you won't communicate well in other ways either.

2   **Opt for simplicity**
    Simplicity is always elegant, whether you're dressing for a casual occasion or a ball. You can't miss making a good impression with a tailored suit or well-cut casual clothes. Make sure your shoes aren't too tight, or, for women, so high that you wobble dangerously with every step.

3   **Make sure you feel comfortable**
    It's most important that you wear clothes in which you feel at ease. You won't come across well, no matter how elegant the clothing, if you're walking around like a store dummy because you're scared to crease your suit, or if you're tugging at a too-tight skirt. Never wear anything that is too tight, too short or too low-cut for the occasion. Trust your instincts!

4   **Choose colours and style carefully**
    Just as the colour of walls and furniture has been shown to have an effect on the well-being of workers, the colours of your clothes can influence both the way you feel and other people's attitudes towards you.

    If a dark business suit and a pastel shirt are expected, you may feel there is little you can do. Not so. People notice more than just colour. Take care to choose a well-cut suit that's expertly made from a quality fabric. And if it's a tad tight, either diet or buy a new suit.

Ties, too, tell a lot more about you than you'd think—paisley is a modern classic; stripes are conservative; a repeated geometric pattern says you're a person who likes structure. Ties with a flower design, an impressionistic or abstract effect, or pictures on them should be kept for when you're entertaining.

Try to avoid pockets bulging with coins, wallets, handkerchiefs, keys and so on. A lumpy look and straining seams do little for your image!

Women have a great deal more leeway. If you're having doubts about what to wear to a formal meeting or function, pick more subdued colours, and lift the effect with accessories. An appointment with a colour consultant is a good investment if you're not sure which colours suit you.

Professional image consultants run courses which you might find helpful. Courses such as these include wardrobe organising, 'selling yourself' with clothes, shopping skills and much more. Even if you have no innate sense of style, you can learn enough to get by. You'll find more information in management magazines and training information brochures. If you *know* you have no clothes sense, a consultant is a good idea.

Before dressing for any occasion, ask yourself these questions:

1 What do others expect of me?
   (Should I dress casually or formally?)
2 What will create the image I want?
   (Clothing fabric, style and colour; accessories—jewellery, scarf, pocket handkerchief, etc.; colour, style and height of shoes.)
3 Do I feel comfortable?
   (With the totality of your appearance: hairstyle, colour scheme, anything you wear or carry.)

Remember that if people are expecting you to look and dress a certain way, and you don't fit their expectations, you run the risk of creating a negative first impression. By following the above guidelines, you can help avoid that.

And here's a final question: If you saw someone walk into a room who looked and dressed as you do, would you want to employ that person?

EYE CONTACT

Eyes are the mirror of the soul.

Most of us aren't confident that we are getting our message across to people, *unless* we can see their eyes. Why is this? What do we see there?

We see warmth, or distance.

We see agreement or disbelief.

We may see scorn, we may see empathy.

Pick up any novel, and you will read lines like:

His stony gaze made the other man falter.

Her eyes danced with laughter.

His smile was not reflected in his eyes.

The last line, particularly, shows how important messages conveyed by the eyes can be. People can tell by your eyes whether you're telling the truth or not.

Eye contact can mean the difference between being believed or not believed; being liked or not liked. When we say that someone had a 'shifty-eyed' look we actually mean that the person made minimal or no eye contact. Most people equate eye contact with honesty, so if you're uneasy about your eye contact, you'd do well to practise.

Of course, there are some spectacularly good liars who use eye contact to fool other people. Charles Dickens put it this way:

I have known a vast quantity of nonsense talked about bad men not looking you in the face. Don't trust that conventional idea. Dishonesty will stare honesty out of countenance any day in the week if there is anything to be got by it.

You also need to take cultural differences into account. Some ethnic groups find excessive eye contact offensive or rude. If in doubt, 'mirror' the other person's behaviour. Use the same amount of eye contact they do—just glance occasionally at their eyes and the rest of the time look over their shoulder or at their forehead.

AVOID NEGATIVITY AND ASSOCIATE WITH POSITIVE PEOPLE

One thing all the top achievers have in common is that they associate with positive people. They know that negativity is their greatest enemy.

Negative thinking stops you from making the most of life's opportunities. You see what could go wrong, instead of the shining possibilities. Negative thinkers are unwilling to take even calculated risks. Why ask for a better job? You won't get it. Why go to the party? You probably won't enjoy it anyway. Why plan a barbecue? It might rain.

Begin to practise positive thinking *now*. Look around you for the positive, cheerful people you know and cultivate friendships with them. In every situation, imagine the best outcome and the worst outcome. Then think only of the best, and concentrate on making it happen.

Life's too short to allow any room for negativity. As the great Dr Murray Banks once said, 'Live every day as though it's your last—and one day you'll be right!'

5

BECOMING A WELL-ROUNDED PERSON

BALANCE YOUR LIFE

Sometimes the reason we don't have much in the way of self-confidence is that our lives lack balance. We're concentrating so hard on building a career that there's no time for anything but work. Or we exercise conscientiously and watch our diets, but forget to feed our minds with new and challenging ideas.

If your life is out of balance, it's probably contributing to a lack of self-confidence. You should aim for a mix of work and pleasure, a life notable for both mental and physical stimulation.

With the changes in our society, there's more danger than ever before of losing sight of the importance of balance. People are working huge hours to save their jobs, thinking that if they do the work of two people they won't be fired. They feel guilty, knowing that their families are being neglected or their fitness level is dropping, but push aside these concerns. They tell themselves that next month, next year, they'll slow down.

Too often, 'next month' never comes. Before they know it, years have gone by dedicated to the great god *Work*. Health, family, relationships, recreation and community activities have fallen by the wayside. They feel both miserable and trapped.

The unpalatable truth is that when things get tight, companies look at the bottom line first and service records second. Employees who have worked themselves into the ground find themselves no better off than colleagues who have made time for other interests.

Resolve now that you won't fall into this trap.

HOLIDAYS

Holidays are essential. A holiday doesn't have to be a cruise or a vacation in some exotic foreign port. It can be as simple as a day when you have a break from work or routine activities. A holiday should be spent doing something you enjoy. It's a reward: a whole day or weekend or week where you can indulge yourself.

The break gives you a chance to recharge your batteries and feel that life's not all work, or an inescapable grind of small children and household tasks. You owe it not only to yourself but also to others who have to interact with you. Taking a break can mean you see the world in a whole new light.

WORK

If you have a job you enjoy, you're very lucky. If the job is not so great, you have the option of changing it or changing your attitudes towards it. Is there anything about your job you can change to make it more enjoyable? Can you delegate onerous tasks? Can you direct your activities into an area which challenges your skills?

Too many people don't think of changing what they *do* in their jobs as an option—the first thing that comes to mind is always, 'I've got to get a *different job*'. You may be surprised at how receptive your boss may be to the idea of you adapting your roles within the company.

For instance, a while ago I finally had a few free hours to visit some old friends. Their daughter, Lenore, was hunched over the Positions Vacant ads with a highlighter pen.

'Hey,' I said in surprise, 'what happened to that job you had? I thought you loved it?'

'I did—*then*,' she said darkly, grabbing some scissors to clip the ads. 'Now I'm bored out of my brain. I can do everything I need to in half a day. I've *got* to get out.'

'From wonderful to boring in three months?' I sat down across from her. 'Surely it's not that bad?'

She silenced me with one of those scathing you-couldn't-possibly-understand looks.

'It's all right for you, Doug. You're always charging off doing fascinating things. Me, I just sit there and file and invoice and organise the office. It was a mess when I started, but it's so well organised now it runs itself. I'm going nuts.'

'What were you hired to do?'

She sighed. 'You're going to say I knew the job description when I started and now I should count my blessings that I've got an easy job and a good boss, right? Mum's already said all that.'

I hadn't been going to say anything of the sort, and I told her so. What I *was* going to say—and did—was that Lenore should do everything she could to develop her skills where she was, rather than snatching at any new job that looked a possibility.

'You've admitted that you've got a good boss,' I said. 'Does he know how you feel?'

'Well, no,' she admitted. She didn't like to hurt his feelings. 'How can I tell him I don't want to do this any more? He's so happy about the office running efficiently at last.'

'Tell him,' I said. 'Not many bosses mind being told that their staff want to take on extra responsibility!'

'But what can I do?'

'Sit down tonight,' I suggested, 'and start by writing down all the things you do now. Write down everything you've done since you started. Then jot down as many different ways as possible that you could become involved in the business. It doesn't matter if other people are doing those jobs right now; we're just looking at what's possible.'

Already she was looking more interested. 'I don't have to just stick to my office jobs?'

'Not for the purposes of this exercise. Finally, write down any special skills and interests you have. If you're interested in some aspect of the business you're not trained for, make a note that you need to *develop* some skills.'

'What if the boss tells me I can't do any of it?'

I groaned. 'First, Lenore, start thinking positively!'

'But what if he says …'

'If you really can't get anywhere,' I said, 'then you still concentrate on developing your own skills, and eventually you will have to get another job. But don't assume the worst before you try it!'

Lenore did what I suggested. Luckily, there are more forward-thinking, flexible bosses out there than the reverse, and Lenore found that her boss was delighted to hear of her interest. Within days the first changes were underway, and Lenore is now happily using her organisational skills in three separate areas. Not only that, she is developing her knowledge by buying the latest books in the field while she is waiting for the next intake in the course of her choice.

Most of us have to spend the greater part of our lives at work. There's nothing more calculated to destroy self-esteem than having to go along to a dreary job, day after day. So if you really hate your job, and have limited avenues open to you within it—change it.

It may take time for you to prepare the skills you need for another job and, admittedly, it's harder to change careers in times of recession. This is where your positive thinking will boost you up and help you through. Instead of moping around thinking, 'Oh, I'd give anything to be in a different field', start making lists or a planning sheet.

Do what Lenore did. List the things you really like doing, and the sorts of things you don't like doing:

★ Do you like to work with people, do you prefer to work quietly at a desk?

★ Do you like to follow instructions and complete a job step by step, or do you like to work independently?

★ To do the kind of job you think you'd really enjoy, do you need to upgrade your skills?

★ Do you need to do a college or university course?

Work is a major part of your life. Don't make the mistake of thinking that you can put up with a rotten job and compensate for it in other areas of your life. That would be like following a dose of castor oil with a sweet. Is that how you want your life to be, five days out of seven, for the next ten, twenty or thirty years?

There are lots of career-planning guides on the market, probably none better than *What Colour is Your Parachute?* by Richard Nelson Bolles (Ten Speed Press, Berkeley, California). This classic is updated annually, and gives you advice on job-hunting, interviews, using your skills, and—probably best of all—a section on deciding what you really want out of life. Buy it, read it, use it.

HEALTH

It's pretty hard to project confidence and enthusiasm if you feel tired, headachy or ill. Nor is it easy to smile and talk when you're breathing hard from heaving fifteen extra kilos up a flight of steps.

You can improve both your physical and mental energy by establishing routines to ensure good health. Mental and emotional well-being improve dramatically with regular exercise, plenty of sleep, and periods of deep relaxation.

There are enough people around ready to lecture you on the importance of keeping fit, so we won't take up a lot of space in this book by repeating the messages that surround you. But *do* take the time to stop and reflect that those messages are there for a reason—there's no getting around it; unhealthy people are at a disadvantage.

Good health is good for you!

★ You look more attractive—and healthy, attractive people automatically get a bigger share of the goodies.

★ You have the energy to cope with stressful situations, ranging from high-pressure deadlines, to job interviews, to making speeches.

★ Your whole outlook becomes more positive. You're one step closer to projecting a positive self-image!

Admittedly, you might have been born with certain conditions that you have to learn to live with: allergic reactions, asthma, a tendency to rheumatics, or perhaps something even more serious. But we can all make the best of what we have. Aim for the best possible state of health you can.

Food can be one of life's greatest pleasures, but it can also make you miserable if you allow it too prominent a role in your life. Regard food primarily as fuel. Food is simply what your body needs to keep it operating at maximum performance. People who care for their cars don't use an inferior brand of oil; keen gardeners choose different foods for different plants; athletes select their food carefully to achieve a balance that will keep their bodies operating at maximum efficiency.

I'm not saying that you should become obsessive about food, but do your body a favour and don't give it too much junk. It'll soon let you know how it feels about that if you do: by piling on the kilos, hitting you with dizzy spells or bouts of breathlessness, or savaging you with headaches or darting pains. It's a bit hard to project a positive self-image with any of that going on!

Health involves a balance of mental and physical activity and rest. For your mind to remain healthy (and positive!) *it* needs to be fed the right food too!

To stimulate your mind:

★ read interesting books and magazines (fiction and non-fiction), including 'how-to' books that will increase your skills and knowledge

★ go to plays and movies and discuss them with friends

★ undertake a course of study in an area of interest to you

★ join a club

★ take up a craft that stimulates your mind.

While we're on the subject of health, think about *laughter* as a magic elixir. It's a tonic. It's a medicine. It's a vitamin. If you haven't enough laughter in your life, do something about it. Scientific studies prove that patients who laugh recover more quickly and have less pain than those who don't. Women's magazines have run surveys and found that women rate a sense of humour in their mates as more important than sex. Find out what tickles your funny bone and go get some of it. Prescribe for yourself a good dose of carefree laughter!

WHAT YOU SAY

Once you have done all you can to create a good first impression by the way you look, you're going to have to back it up by what you *say*. This may be where some of you begin to quail.

Maybe you're quite happy with the way you *look*. You're not too bad at coordinating your wardrobe, you're always well groomed, and you're in fairly good health. But *talk* to people? Oh, no. You're too shy. You're worried you'll wreck everything if you open your mouth. You don't know what to say to others! You don't know how to keep a conversation going!

Join the club.

There are many, many people out there who feel just the way you do. They agonise over talking to strangers at parties or seminars. They would rather die than speak in front of a group. Communication with others seems like one big mystery.

Apart from what to say, how to say it, and when to say it, you may be worried about other aspects of your speech. Maybe you're self-conscious because you're aware that your speech is not grammatically correct. People might have picked you up on it a few times. Or perhaps you're not used to expressing yourself, and you can't find the right word when you want it.

It's true that other people make judgements about you on the basis of your overall appearance and demeanour. However, the minute you open your mouth, their first impressions are either set in concrete or revised. *What you say* and *how you say it* are of great importance. How can you make sure you give people the right impression of who you are?

WHAT TO SAY, HOW TO SAY IT, WHEN TO SAY IT

Just as your expression causes people to label you as scared, condescending or whatever, the first words you speak will have their mental gears meshing instantly to categorise you further. If those first words make you sound nasty, stupid or dishonest, that's the way you'll be remembered.

Here are a few tips about how to make those first words count.

1 Speak first

Take the initiative and open up the lines of communication. Just be friendly: a brief 'Hello—I'm Mary Smith' will do to start. It's likely that the other person will be vastly relieved. They're probably just as shy and uncertain as you are, *even if they don't show it*. Now the ball's in their court.

2 Speak slowly

Don't underestimate the importance of speaking slowly. If you speak too quickly, people have trouble understanding you. Besides, speaking slowly enables you to make better use of *pauses* and *eye contact*—two proven ways of communicating better with people.

3 Ask questions

Even in a workshop situation or a business meeting, it's a mistake to think that you need to get right down to business. What you have to do first is bridge the gap between you—and the best way to do that is by asking questions that are designed to draw expansive answers. Ask open-ended questions which will establish contact between you and the other person.

4   Learn to listen

Many people have problems with communicating because they worry too much about what *they* are going to say, rather than listening to what the speaker is saying. Asking questions to develop rapport is a good technique. But it won't work if you don't listen with interest to the replies. Good listening involves two basic behaviours. First, *look* at the speaker the whole time they are speaking. Second, *provide feedback*: nods, smiles, or more questions based on what has already been said. If you really listen and take an interest in what someone is saying, the questions will come naturally and easily—and so will true communication!

5   Overcome poor grammar/impoverished vocabulary

If you're worried either about poor grammar or not being able to find the right word, there are steps you can take to fix the problem. What you must realise is that *you won't fix it overnight*. Like most people who embark on self-improvement programs, you'll probably want everything to happen yesterday, but life's not like that!

This is what you can do:

* Read, read, read! Most people with a good vocabulary armed themselves with those wonderful words by being keen readers. Read the papers, read magazines, read books and more books. When you come across words you don't know or are uncertain of how to use, write them in a notebook. Look them up in the dictionary. Write them in a sentence and see if you can work them into the conversation. But don't go overboard with all this! Who wants a reputation for spouting big words that either sound pretentious or leave people looking blank? Always remember: *words should foremost express, not simply impress*.
* When describing events or films to people, try to use interesting, expressive language instead of common slang or overused words.
* Buy some basic books on grammar and work through the exercises. However, if you read widely, you will 'absorb' correct grammar to some extent.
* Ask close friends or workmates to tell you if you are using incorrect grammar.

6   Be positive

You've probably heard this one before, but let's try a different angle. Instead of worrying about how you can make other people think you are positive and optimistic, turn the spotlight on them. If you make an effort to focus on the things in other people which might be worthy of a compliment, you'll be on track for a positive approach. Projecting a positive image to the world around you will be a cinch—and you won't even have to work at it!

It's very easy to pick up a person's attitude to the world. Sure, we all know there are problems in the world—but nobody wants to hear about them. Focus on the positive all the time in your own personality. And look for the positive in other people.

TO BOOST YOUR OWN SELF-CONFIDENCE, BOOST OTHERS

Ralph Waldo Emerson once said, '*The measure of mental health is the disposition to find good everywhere*'. It sounds almost too simple to be true, but psychologists and behavioural scientists have found it to be so over and over again. If you make an effort to give others a boost, your own self-confidence automatically soars as well!

Why does this happen? There are all sorts of subconscious reasons. For a start, if you make others feel better about themselves, you are wielding some sort of power. *You* have something others want—a reassuring word, a vote of confidence. Your subconscious mind thinks, 'Well, I sure made his day. I'm good for something!' or perhaps, 'I feel really happy my opinion makes such a difference.'

Looking for good in others, or ways to build others up, takes our minds off ourselves. By making us feel less self-conscious, it helps our self-image. It makes us less self-righteous and more tolerant.

You probably know one or two unhappy people. You're likely to find that they tend to be very critical—of people's habits, their lifestyles, their possessions, their clothes. You name it, they find something to criticise!

Naturally you don't want people to see *you* as a carping critic, so if you do feel unhappy, watch yourself closely for signs of over-zealous fault-finding.

Super-critical people commonly use sentences starting with:

* I hate it when …
* She/he never …
* Trust Jane X to always …
* He/she should …
* If I've told you once, I've told you a thousand times …

You can see the pattern—things are never right!

If this sounds a little bit too much like you for comfort, please don't use it as another club to beat yourself with! Recognition of a problem is the first step towards solving it. You can take steps to combat negativity. The main thing to keep in mind is that *if you boost others, you boost yourself*. It does work.

Try these simple actions:

* When you want to criticise, look for something to praise instead. Never find fault if you can point out the good. Often, people will feel such goodwill towards you that they'll fix whatever was wrong without your having to say anything!

* When you do praise someone, make sure it's sincere. Praise *what a person has done* rather than the person—you get better results when people know what they're being praised for.

* Before you jump in and say something you can't take back, think to yourself, 'Other people have needs and anxieties too'.

* When you're ready to charge ahead and do things *your* way, back off a bit and put yourself in the other person's shoes. How would you feel in their position?

* Listen actively to what others say. This means suspending judgements and opinions so you really hear what is being said. This way you open the channels of communication.

YOUR BUSINESS IMAGE VERSUS YOUR PRIVATE IMAGE

Every so often, you read about people in public life—especially politicians—who have 'an image problem'. They come across as being too arrogant, or spineless, or too decorative (as opposed to useful). Quite often, it's simply a matter of them feeling uncomfortable in front of a microphone or a camera. Away from the media, these people have friends who see them as warm, caring, hard-working people.

Many of us have the same problem in relation to our image at work and our image at home. We may be cheerful, contented people at home, appreciated by our families and confident in our ability to manage a home and relate to the family. Then we go to work and everything falls apart. It becomes harder to 'project' the real person inside. We feel we have to act a part: be aggressive, or subservient, or show leadership qualities, or prove ourselves again and again. We seem to walk around in some kind of shell.

Some people react by becoming aggressive. 'I've got to take the lead or nothing ever gets done around here.' Others become withdrawn and do the bare minimum. 'It doesn't matter what I do, I can't seem to please the boss—so I'll just do as much as I have to, to get my paycheck.'

The problem is that the two roles we play aren't in harmony. People often feel like this when they get onto the corporate treadmill: you have to do things the accepted way or someone stomps on your head.

What can you do about it? Well, if you've misrepresented your talents or qualifications in the first place to get the job, you've bought a pack of trouble. You can:

1   try to get out of it by admitting you're not suited to the work and ask for a transfer to a different position or department
2   retrain and upgrade your skills to increase your confidence
3   put up with it and hope it gets better
4   quit!

Option 3 is not recommended. Can you see why? Because you're taking a passive role. If you want to build your self-confidence and start projecting that confidence, you need to be taking an active role in your own life. (Remember what I said about lack of choice being one of the factors contributing to low self-esteem?)

To feel good about yourself, you need to take the initiative and become a partner in your own destiny in *all areas* of your life. You'll be happiest when your private image and your business image blend—and when they match your idea of what you want to be like.

In a nutshell, you will be working on every aspect of your life at the same time. There's no need to be rash about it, of course. Nobody expects you to toss in your job, divorce your spouse, farm out your children and go into retreat for a year to 'find yourself'!

Just sit down, take a good long look at your life and what you want from it, and start a workable plan to become the person your inner self tells you is right for you.

SELLING YOUR IMAGE

Projecting a positive self-image means that you are, in a way, 'selling' yourself to other people. You can see the logic of this. If you recognise the need to develop your personality, then you are already aware that, as a human being, you are a kind of product. You want to market yourself to others in the best possible light. The idea is to learn how to sell yourself and ask the right price.

You may find the prospect of improving your self-image exciting in some ways and very difficult in others, because you must take some risks. Change takes time, but anyone can do it if they have the motivation to improve.

I once ran a training seminar for some of this country's top footballers. The aim was to get across to them the idea that top professional athletes need also to ensure that they are top communicators. Top products need top packaging.

I could see that these athletes were having difficulty identifying with this statement. Their first passion was in place: their love of and commitment to their sport. Who wanted to *talk* about it as well? Wasn't it enough that they were giving the fans what they came to the matches to see?

'In today's competitive world,' I asked them, 'what is the life of a top-grade league player?'

They looked at each other, then finally one of them volunteered, 'About seven years'.

I said, 'What happens to you after you've been in the limelight for that period—then nothing?'

Silence reigned.

'Now,' I said, 'let's think of a player who has managed to marry his professional skills with his personality and has developed his communication skills. Where is he now?'

'Television,' they chorused.

Bingo. The idea was planted.

The message is there not only for professional athletes, but everyone who wants to make a success of their lives. Train yourself now for your next stop. Become an experienced being, not a has-been.

THE UNIVERSITY OF LIFE

Are you ready to start the development of self? There's no better school than the University of Life—and expert teachers are everywhere. You will find 'lessons' in a variety of places:

* ★ books
* ★ tapes
* ★ movies

★ people
★ workshops
★ seminars.

I met a young person who was so depressed about his circumstances that you could almost see the lights go off when he entered a room.

He was bored with his lifestyle, he confided. Everyone else seemed to be having all the fun.

'Change is difficult for all of us,' I said. I told him of the words of the great international lecturer, Bill Gove, 'If things are to change, *we* have to change'. I gave him a copy of Dale Carnegie's classic book *How to Win Friends and Influence People*.

He couldn't wait to read it. And once he had, it turned around the way he felt about life. He took a big step and went to a weekend workshop on dress, where he learnt to visualise himself as a package that needed to be wrapped. He invested $1500 in upmarket clothes, and his outlook continued to change and grow. Now, two years later, he walks into a room and the lights go *on*!

Now you can do the same. What changes can you initiate to make the lights go on in *your* life?

6

THE TOP TEN CONVERSATIONAL MISTAKES

Ordinary conversation gives you many opportunities to perfect your skills in relating to others. You should regard every conversation as an opportunity to show people who you are—or the 'you' you want to be. Yet many people dread making conversation with anyone other than close friends or family. Why?

The main reason most people are afraid to strike up a conversation with others is that they are *afraid of rejection*. They're worried that they will somehow seem inadequate. What if they say something stupid? What if the other person is bored? What do you talk about after the weather? And what if the other person doesn't want to talk about the weather!

Don't worry so much! A friend of mine, Harry, once told me, 'You know, I used to hate going through all that small talk when you first met someone. I thought it was all false; stilted. Then I realised it was more like an orchestra warming up before the performance—or a racing car revving its engines on the starting grid. You can't leap straight into the main action.'

Instantly I saw how right he was. You have to give people a chance to absorb information about you, before overwhelming them with Deep and Meaningfuls. 'Hi! How are you? Dreadful weather we're having' may sound trite, but it gives the other person time to mentally classify all sorts of things about you. They have to process clues from body language, accent, apparent level of education, and so on.

People often run into trouble with a conversation because they are preoccupied with what the other person thinks of them. Often they start 'acting a part' to impress the listener, instead of trying to relate to them. If you make a deliberate attempt to impress, you will be so self-conscious that you will run the risk of sounding pretentious instead. The best advice, in order for you to create the best impression, is to *be as natural as possible*. Breathe slowly (some people have the opposite problem: they're so nervous they forget to breathe!) and make a conscious effort to relax muscles.

What if you're so overcome with shyness or fear that you're virtually paralysed? If you can't think of a single interesting thing to say?

You should be thinking of the other person, not yourself. Remember: everyone wants to be liked by other people. It's simple to overcome that paralysis. Get other people talking about themselves. They'll go away thinking what a brilliant conversationalist you are.

People become much more receptive to *you* and your ideas if they've had a chance to express themselves first. If you think about it, you'll realise that we humans are all innately selfish. We tend to think about how things will affect *us* first, others second. Our own problems, love affairs, career and so forth always seem infinitely more interesting and important than those of other people.

Knowing this, it's simple to keep a conversation going. Draw the other person out. If *invited* to speak about yourself, do so—briefly. Treat a conversation like a tennis match: the other person serves, you return the ball, there's a volley, then if the ball goes out of the court (or the conversation about *them* peters out) it's *your* turn to serve.

It's easier to develop a natural, easy conversational style if you are aware of the things that turn people off: the 'conversation stoppers'.

Here they are, the Top Ten.

1   NOT LISTENING

You might be *hearing* what the other person has to say—but are you really *listening*?

There *is* a difference! If you are really listening to what someone is saying, you hear not only the words but the emotional messages *behind* the words. In fact, a skilful and empathetic listener will often realise that what someone is saying is not necessarily what they really mean.

To be a good listener, you should:

★ Push aside any other matters which preoccupy you, and concentrate on the other person's message.

★ Listen with genuine interest and caring. Focus more on the person behind the message than on the words you hear. Look for a point of contact with the other person, an overlapping of interests.

★ Avoid being distracted by loud music, a TV show, or other people.

★ Learn to look for, and overcome, negative attitudes in yourself when it comes to listening to other people. Try not to display any sort of prejudice or lack of interest.

★ Don't take offence too easily. If you think you're being insulted, check first to see whether the other person's message is what you thought it was. It is very easy to misunderstand words or intentions.

To be a good listener, the most important thing you should remember is this: *you need to focus on the other person.*

2   NEGATIVE STATEMENTS

Things never work out for me.

People always let me down.

Of course it won't work.

Negative statements drag down so many conversations. Try an experiment. For 24 hours, count the number of negative statements you hear from others. In addition, make a real effort to eliminate negativity from your own words! It's harder than you might think.

Negative statements are sure conversation-stoppers—especially if you're chatting to upbeat people. You'll find they'll drift away rather than talk to you for too long. Think positively. Speak positively. That way you attract positive people, and everyone feels better!

3   FAILING TO RESPOND

I've never met anyone yet who likes talking to a brick wall. Unfortunately I've encountered many people who give a good impression of being one! It goes without saying that it's not much fun talking to someone who doesn't respond. Lack of response can take two forms:

★ The person mumbles 'yes' or 'no' or 'mmm', smiles weakly into their mineral water and lets the silence stretch out until *you* pick up the conversation again.

★ The person can't wait for you to finish so they can dismiss your comments with a careless 'How interesting', before embarking upon their own favourite topic of conversation (often themselves).

If you want to be a good conversationalist, *respond* to the other person's words. More specifically, respond to the feelings behind the words.

4   INTERRUPTING

Always pay people the courtesy of letting them finish what they are saying. Yes, you can run into difficulties if you get saddled with the town bore, the type who doesn't ever draw breath long enough for you to respond. With this person you may have to butt in with an excuse to remove yourself from their presence—permanently.

With most people, however, the rule is: *don't interrupt*. It's frustrating to be trying to talk to someone who is continually trying to finish your sentences or jumps in to give their opinion before you've had time to finish your story.

Ever been in a conversation that goes something like this?

PERSON A:	'I was on my way to that new supermarket yesterday when — '
PERSON B:	'The one on Radburne Street! Oh, I went there just the other day myself! Bought some great bargain shoes.'
PERSON A:	'Yes, that one. Anyway, I was only a block from home when this car came round the corner — '
PERSON B:	'Don't tell me! You had an accident!'
PERSON A:	'No, I was going to say, I saw the driver was that new fitness instructor at — '
PERSON B:	' — the Trim 'n' Fit Gym!'

… and so on!

If you're the poor sod trying to tell the story, such interruptions wear thin very quickly indeed. In fact, you're likely to avoid encounters with the other person whenever possible, because conversations are such hard work. Respond, yes. Interrupt, *no*!

5   ARROGANT ASSERTIONS

What's your reaction when someone points a finger at you and starts a sentence with 'Mark my words …'? Do your hackles tend to rise just a tiny bit? Can you feel your teeth grinding?

Not many of us like being told what to think. We like to think we are independent enough to have our own opinions and draw our own conclusions.

If you want to win people over, don't make arrogant assertions. It's quite possible they disagree with you, in which case you've alienated them from the start. Besides, you'll look pretty stupid if you're wrong!

In a conversation, be prepared to discuss, not make assertions.

6   STRAYING FROM THE POINT

Ever noticed a dog's paw tracks on sand or through mud? If you tried to follow those tracks, you'd be walking in a lot of circles. Dogs tend to trot along for a bit; stop to investigate a new smell; backtrack; sniff at something else; detour down an inviting little lane … There are tempting diversions everywhere and no direct route from A to B.

Some people conduct a conversation in the same way. A stray word here sparks a memory there; they detour to tell another story; they collect themselves ('… Now, what was I talking about before I got on to Jack's new car? Oh yes, Mary's promotion, that was it …') and then detour again ('… which reminds me, don't let me forget to tell you about Paul's fight with the boss …')

Stick to the point! Apart from anything else, long meandering stories tend to be monologues rather than conversations. Give the other person a chance for feedback—and an opportunity to tell their story.

Another mistake related to taking detours along the conversational path is the 'potted history'. There's nothing drearier than listening to someone who takes an age to 'set the scene'. By the time they get to the punch line the audience is asleep.

7 ARGUING

Some people just *love* a good argument. They're ready to challenge you on any point. Unfortunately, if you're a peaceable type, you'll tend to feel as though you've been cornered by a starving Doberman.

If you're trapped by a 'fighter', smile and nod a lot. Refuse to get drawn into an argument. They'll be bored with you in about five minutes flat, and push off to find someone with a bit more 'spark'—someone else who's spoiling for a fight.

If, on the other hand, *you* are the argumentative type, learn to cool it. Even if you think you're right, don't argue. No one wins arguments *or* friends by arguing.

Most of us are not either fighters or pacifists. We fall into the middle range. Just occasionally, we're tempted to disagree with people or—especially if we *know* we're right—to point out their mistakes.

Don't do it. Remember: people *dislike* those who disagree with them, and they *don't* like being disagreed with.

What should you do if you can't agree with people? Simple: just don't disagree with them, unless it's really necessary—and this, you'll find, doesn't happen very often.

8 'BEARER OF GLOOM'

I know of a woman who puts off visiting her mother as long as possible. The reason? The conversation is one long catalogue of woes. Someone has just died from cancer. Someone else has just had the most terrible run of bad luck. The neighbours are not speaking to her.

By the time my friend finally escapes, she feels a heavy cloud of gloom hanging over her head as well.

Here is a piece of advice. Write this on a small card and put it in your wallet:

No scars

No scars? What does that mean?

It's a timely reminder not to show your 'scars' to other people—that is, don't tell them about your operations, your financial problems, your illness, your souring love affair or how you hate the opposite sex.

People don't want to hear about your troubles.

When people say, 'How are you?' it's normally not an invitation to describe your state of health. It's a gambit to open a conversation. If you take it at face value and start telling them about every ache and pain and last night's bout of insomnia, their eyes will glaze over and the conversation is D-E-A-D, *dead!*

9 CRITICISING/COMPLAINING ABOUT OTHERS

A golden rule for discussing other people is this: *If you can't say something good, say nothing.* Criticism has a habit of coming back to bite the critic. You're bound to have heard the comment 'So-and-so never has a good word to say about anyone'.

If people often hear you criticise or complain about others, they'll never really trust you. How do they know you won't be complaining about them to someone else one day?

Remember, you can never make yourself look good by making other people look bad. Your progress in the world will be determined by your own efforts and worth. If you can find absolutely nothing good to say about someone else, change the topic of conversation. Stay positive.

A variant of criticising or complaining about other people is teasing the person to whom you are talking. This in itself can be a thinly veiled form of criticism. If you want to keep the lines of communication open, be very careful about teasing people. Where, exactly, is the division between humour and sarcasm? Where is the line between teasing and bullying?

Many of us can recall being absolutely devastated by treatment from an older brother or sister or so-called friends, who would say with an air of great injury later, 'I don't know what you're getting so upset about! I was only kidding. You just can't take it.'

If you 'tease' someone, you may be the only one having a good time. Don't ever run the risk of threatening someone's self-esteem. Nobody appreciates cheap shots.

10 TALKING ABOUT YOURSELF

What is the number one thing people are interested in?

Themselves.

We are all vitally interested in our *own* journey through life! That's natural. And that's why you must keep in mind at all times that the chief interest of the person you're talking to is *not* you and your concerns.

Whether you're chatting to someone or making a speech, the paramount consideration should be what interests your audience, not what interests you. Talk about yourself, and they'll be likely to consider you a self-centred bore. And they'll be right.

So there you are. *The Top Ten conversational mistakes.* Get to know what they are and avoid them like the plague if you want to be a successful communicator. Here they are again, in a handy, never-to-be-forgotten list:

1   Not listening
2   Negative statements
3   Failing to respond
4   Interrupting
5   Arrogant assertions
6   Straying from the point
7   Arguing
8   'Bearer of gloom'
9   Criticising/complaining about others
10   Talking about yourself.

7

THE PF FACTOR

Have you ever wondered why we keep dogs as pets? For most people the family dog is a constant source of problems and irritations. It persecutes the postie. It kills the neighbours' cat on the living room rug while the family is watching television. It digs up your flowers. It piddles on your shrubs. It costs you a fortune in dog food and vet's fees.

Why bother?

Wouldn't it be better to find a good home for it with a family of masochists? They'd love it.

Well, you might be interested to know that a recent study showed that when adults talk to other human beings their blood pressure usually rises. But when they talk to their pet dog—their blood pressure goes down by 10 per cent.

And do you know why?

People judge! Dogs don't!

That's at least one reason to keep old Fido. He makes you feel good. He accepts you as you are. He is always grateful when you do something for him. And he shows it!

There's a lesson in relating to people here. If you want people to respond to you, if you want to find conversational skills easy, if you want to project a warm, positive personality at work and at home—use Fido as a model of good communication.

Let me explain.

Most people never think about communication. We can all talk, can't we? So we can all communicate.

Right?

Actually, it's more like playing the violin. If you're an expert you make it look easy. You produce beautiful music. People stop to listen. They smile. They feel good.

But if your technique stinks and you haven't practised much, playing the violin is a great way of emptying a room.

Communication is the same. Good communicators effortlessly establish mutually satisfying contacts with other people. Poor communicators drive people away.

If you want to relate well to people, you can't afford to be a poor communicator. You have to consider what you need to do in order to establish productive relationships, whether it's with the people you supervise at work, an audience or someone you've just met. You need to become conscious of the PF factor: the *positive feedback factor*.

Here's what it means.

Remember when you started work for the first time? You probably weren't always sure about how well you were doing in your job. Can you remember an occasion when the boss called you aside and said something like, 'I just want to tell you how pleased we are with your work. You're a real asset to the firm. Thank you for your efforts.'

If you can remember an incident like that you're one of the lucky ones. The truth is that most of the feedback given by managers and supervisors to staff is *negative*. That is the single greatest problem in Australian business management today. The bosses behave as fault-finders and error-detectors. They only react to mistakes.

You may or may not be in a supervisory position at this stage. But the PF factor works at all levels. Think about your workmates. How would they react if you said something like, 'It's great working with someone who's so well organised' or 'You did a good job on that submission' or 'Mary, your sense of humour brightens my day!'?

Everyone responds to positive feedback. They start to share ideas, suggest plans for future action, and feel encouraged to show initiative.

Here's a true story about the way the *positive feedback factor* works.

Back in the late 1950s, a young man got a job as a clerk with one of the big insurance companies in Sydney. He was just one among dozens of clerks in the firm. But the assistant manager in Max's department was observant. He noticed that Max was interested and enthusiastic and energetic. So Phil, the assistant manager, told Max that he liked his work. Max tried even harder. He read the insurance schedules until he knew them backwards. He really got to know about the product his company sold.

Then Phil had an idea. He put Max in a ground-floor office to handle the people who came to the city to renew their policies. He told him that it would be all right to do a bit of selling too: 'Are you aware that this policy doesn't cover attack by killer cockroaches? Can I show you some possible alternatives to your current policy? Is there anything I can do for you?'

Well, Max learnt very quickly. He generated a surprising volume of new business in his ground-floor office. And Phil told him how well he was doing. Of course Max knew that, but that isn't the point, is it?

Pretty soon Phil persuaded the general manager to take a risk. They put Max out on the road as the youngest insurance inspector in the business.

What happened? Did Max use the company car for drag races at the beach? Did he disgrace himself by getting drunk during the day while dealing with clients?

He did not!

He worked hard and he succeeded. Because that move to the ground-floor office had done a lot of important things to him.

First, it showed Max that his boss had confidence in him. Second, it gave him the opportunity to learn about his strengths. He discovered that he was good at selling and he gained knowledge that he would need at the next stages of his career. But most important of all, he developed a belief in his ability to succeed.

Today Max is at the top management level in one of Australia's largest and most successful insurance companies. If you asked him, he'd tell you how much he owes to Phil. It's not a question of native ability: Max had plenty of that. But Phil's positive feedback provided the circumstances that allowed native ability to develop into mature talent.

It really does work. People who believe they can succeed will never stop trying. They'll always give their best.

If you help people to discover their talents, to value themselves and to believe in the possibility of success, you'll be welcomed wherever you go—whether as an employee, manager, parent, spouse, friend, business acquaintance, public speaker or dinner guest! You'll be known as some-one with a warm, positive personality and as a great communicator.

Let's get back to Fido for a moment, because I really wasn't joking when I suggested that you should use the family dog as a model of good communication. Now obviously Fido's conversation skills are limited. But he always shows people that he likes and values them. He lowers their blood pressure and raises their self-esteem.

You could do worse than follow his example.

But it actually goes further. Research studies in the United States have shown that the family member who gets the greatest volume of positive feedback is—you've guessed it—the dog. It gets back what it gives. It gives loyalty and affection, and it gets loyalty and affection back.

So be like Fido. Give loyalty, acknowledgement and support and you'll get them back. Negative feedback destroys. But positive feedback creates an atmosphere of mutual trust, and a sense of shared purpose. You'll become a great communicator, and project a warm, empathetic per-sonality to anyone you meet. And they won't mind nearly as much if you dig up their flower beds and piddle on their shrubs.

Try this quick quiz to assess the amount of feedback you give others:

★ Do you pay compliments?

★ Do you speak clearly?

★ Do you acknowledge what other people are trying to say?

★ Do you explain tactfully and clearly where a person is going off course?

★ Do you look for creative solutions to other people's problems?

★ Do you give credit to people for their ideas?

★ Do you praise effort, creativity and innovative ideas?

★ Do you compliment people on their strengths in front of others?

If you answered 'no' to any of these, there's room for improvement in the amount of positive feedback you give to others in your life.

PART III

EFFECTIVE SPEAKING

8

SPEAK WITH CONFIDENCE—ANYWHERE!

By now, your head should be buzzing with ideas about powering up your people skills. Perhaps you're well on the way already, making changes as you work your way through this book. Whatever stage you're at, one thing is certain. Once people start to notice the new, confident you, you're going to be more in demand. You'll be asked to participate in more events, to lead more activities, to take more responsibility. And as sure as night follows day, you'll be asked to express your views to a wider audience. In other words, *speak in public*.

Was that a nauseated groan I heard? Or just the sound of a plummeting stomach?

Or maybe you're one of the lucky ones who don't actually *fear* public speaking—you'd just like a few hints on how to cope with it. Fine. Stick around.

But if you *are* one of the I'd-rather-die-than-speak-in-public types (far more common) then there's good news ahead. It's not half as difficult as you might expect. So you stick around, too. You're sure to learn something to your advantage.

To start with, I'm going to let you in on a secret.

As your self-esteem starts to grow and your new confidence emerges, the thought of speaking to a group of people won't seem nearly so frightening. In fact, you're more than likely to sit there at seminars or conferences and think, 'I could do that', or even 'I could do *better* than that!'

And it's true.

Everyone you see involved in public speaking has had to learn the craft. They weren't born knowing how to do it. Some may be luckier than others: they might have had parents involved in public life, or they might have been encouraged at school to try out for the debating team. They learnt early that it's entirely possible to speak and have people want to listen to you.

But the only advantage they have over you is that they have a head start. It doesn't mean they're any better.

You can learn to speak confidently in public. And if you become confident in your ability to express yourself in any situation—social, business or personal—then you are more likely to be successful in all your relationships.

Meanwhile, are you still sitting there stubbornly saying, 'But I'm not interested in speaking in front of people. I just want to know how to have a good personality and how to get on with people!'?

I understand how you can feel that way now. But as you start becoming more and more popular because of those warm, empathetic people skills you have developed, people will expect more from you. They will want you to become part of more things—to share yourself with others. That's just the way it works.

Your growth in effective public speaking is likely to be gradual, so I'll outline the main steps involved. That will make it easier for you to see how you can build on your public speaking skills one step at a time. No frightening leaps into the dark!

I've talked a lot about conversational skills. So let's take the next step—refining those conversational skills for effective communication at work. The basics are the same; you just adapt the approach a little. First, I'll look at the five steps to good communication, then relate them to listening skills. Put these skills into operation at work, and guess what will happen? You'll become known as a skilled communicator. And that's when someone will ask you to try communicating to a wider audience.

It will probably start off in a small way. Let's say your boss has increasing confidence in your ability to deal with people. She calls you in and says something like, 'I think you'd be a good person to sit in on this meeting. I have a feeling you could work well with this client.'

So you find yourself sitting in on that meeting. Then more meetings. Gradually, you will become involved in more and more projects.

And what is the logical extension of this? Two things:

★ You might be asked to give a short presentation.
★ You might be asked to train other staff.

These are opportunities that you can't afford to miss. They are an indication that someone is showing confidence in you and your abilities.

It doesn't take a genius to see how things develop from here. Small meetings grow into larger meetings. One client turns into a string of clients. And short presentations can grow into talks in front of larger and larger groups—until one day, you could find yourself the keynote speaker at a conference.

But don't panic. This doesn't all happen overnight. You will find, in fact, that it all happens quite painlessly. After all, you will only be asked to talk about things you know, or give presentations within your area of expertise.

Get this firmly fixed within your mind: people will only invite you to speak because they think you can do it. Because they have confidence in your ability. Because they *like* you! Being asked to speak is a tremendous vote of confidence.

This part of the book will show you, step by step, how to invest even more in your new, confident self. It will show you how to build your confidence and speaking skills until you have no problem with speaking in front of large groups.

Confidence in speaking is not a gift for a fortunate few. It is a skill—and skills can be learnt.

That's why you'll find a chapter entitled 'A Recipe for Success', which lists the simple ingredients necessary for an effective speech, whether you're speaking to three people or three hundred. Following that is a chapter on how to *enjoy* giving presentations—because a presentation is quite likely to be your first experience in public speaking. And they actually *can* be enjoyable!

Finally, there's a chapter on speaking for fun—with a few hints on how to put together a speech at short notice.

Armed with these proven, reliable methods, there's no reason to fear speaking in public. Just relax—and let those people skills come through.

Before we move on, let's take a look at what you have to gain by developing your word power.

1   It's a smart career move

I'm thinking 'career' in the broadest sense of the word here, because excellent skills in oral communication will see you among the leaders in whatever career you choose.

And I mean *any career*: butcher, baker or candlestick maker. Being able to put words together in order to express exactly what you mean will see you make a success of anything.

You will be able to promote your business; express your views in a staff meeting; speak up at parent–teacher nights; market your products. You will be able to negotiate anything from the purchase of a fridge to a wage rise or a promotion.

How often have you listened to someone else skilfully persuading others to subscribe to their point of view and thought enviously, 'I wish I could do that'?

Just look around you at work, in parent groups, at social gatherings. Who are the successful ones, the prime movers and shakers? Most often, they are the ones who can speak confidently in front of others.

2   It will enhance your self-esteem

The more you gain confidence in projecting your personality, the more you boost your self-esteem. But there's nothing like the charge of excitement that you get from standing in front of others—and knowing that they are all focused totally on *you* and what *you* have to say.

With every successful presentation your skills will grow. In an amazingly short time you will forget what it was like to dread speaking in front of a group.

Yes, that charge of adrenalin will always be there. So will the odd butterfly. But that's okay: they're necessary to generate the energy for a top performance. As soon as you begin to speak, the anxiety will drain away.

And you will walk away thinking, 'I *can* do it. I really can!'

3   You will gain experience and contacts in a wider field

When you start to speak in public, you begin to meet people from a wide range of backgrounds. This is a tremendous advantage to you both in business and socially. You have more of a perspective on where you fit into the business world. You will make contacts that will be enormously useful to you in getting your job done.

Every successful business person knows the importance of networking. Many of the great career opportunities come from hearing about an opening through a mutual acquaintance. By becoming known for your skill in public speaking, you are quite likely to be offered a different (and possibly better) job, opportunities to speak to different audiences and increased opportunities in your own area of expertise.

This happened to a young woman who came along to a one-day seminar I ran, 'How to Deliver a Dynamic Presentation'. I met her again ten months later. She was so excited about the way her career was developing she had to come up and tell me about it.

'Hi, Doug. I know you probably won't remember me, but I'm Jenny,' she said, 'and I came to your Dynamic Presentation seminar, almost a year ago.' She shook hands. 'I just wanted to tell you what's been happening since I got the courage to get up and speak …'

Jenny had found an exciting new job, and it had come about because she had worked hard on her public speaking techniques. 'I was originally sent on your course because my boss wanted me to run a staff training course on time management,' she said. 'He liked my methods of organisation. After a while I ended up running courses on both time management and general organisational skills.'

'Let me guess,' I said. 'Someone else heard of you or saw you?'

'Yep,' she said, laughing. 'I ran the courses in all the other branches of the company, and then I did a presentation at a conference. And someone offered me another job!'

Jenny is on the way up—fast. Her new job is in training, and she is starting to speak at more conferences. She can see new opportunities opening up everywhere. But as she said, she wouldn't have believed herself capable of it twelve months before.

Jenny did it, and you can do it. Just one step at a time.

BUILD EXPERIENCE, STEP BY STEP

The key to building up your experience and your confidence in public speaking is to *master each step before going on to the next.*

I often tell people that the way to make yourself grow is to force yourself out of your comfort zone—but I don't advocate a suicidal leap! The last thing I would advise you to do is to take on something you're not ready for.

But *do* be ready for new experiences.

Tackle your progress in these easy steps:

1   Be as good as you can at what you are doing now.

2   Decide on the next step you want to take, and prepare yourself thoroughly for it. Rehearse it privately, rehearse it mentally. Do your homework. Then *have a go*.

3   When that new goal has been reached, stay there until you feel a sense of mastery. But all the time, be looking around and planning your next move. (Plenty of people have used 'not being ready' as an excuse to stagnate forever.) When you know you're ready, s-t-r-e-t-c-h yourself to reach the next goal.

Always look for opportunities. When you find them, take a deep breath and say with confidence, 'Yes, I can do that!'

9

FROM BUSINESS COMMUNICATION TO PUBLIC SPEAKING

The communication skills you develop in social exchanges transfer readily to the business world. And the communication skills needed in running a home and bringing up a family are similar to those used in any business outside the home. You still need to instruct, adjudicate, negotiate, explain, praise, and so on.

BUSINESS COMMUNICATION

Here are five steps to good one-on-one communication:

1 Give people your attention. Let them know that you are a friendly person, that you're interested in them and would like to help them.
2 Feed them 'positive vibes' and try to identify with their concerns *quickly*.
3 If they need information, offer help to the best of your ability. Put it in terms that they can understand. Give the impression that you are a helpful person.
4 Show by your attitude and responses that you are a competent, reliable person.
5 Demonstrate that they can *trust* you with their concerns. No trust—no business. No trust—no relationship.

Remember:

★ It's not how you see yourself, it's how others see you!
★ It's not what you've got, it's what you do with it!

Listening skills are an essential part of the communication process. Listening is sometimes known as 'white magic' because of its effectiveness in solving disputes and engendering good feeling. It shows the speaker that you empathise with them; you understand them.

In the business world, you'll find that if people talk enough, they'll find it impossible to hide their real feelings or motives. In many cases, you can trust your instincts. When you're trying to read someone's mood, your first reaction is often the most reliable.

Often I'll be talking to someone about a business deal, and I'll see smiles and positive nods. Their words sound positive, too. But I feel uneasy: something tells me this person is not convinced, that I've lost the sale.

What's happening is that I'm subconsciously picking up minute signals that say the opposite of the surface signals, the words and smiles. While their words say, 'Yes, I probably do need something like that', their body may be turned away from me. While they smile and nod, their fingers are drumming a silent tattoo against their thighs, or there's a pinched look about their nostrils. They make little or no eye contact.

I might not notice these things on a conscious level, but *subconsciously* I'm picking it all up, filing it away, and my mind sends the message, 'This person's going to say no'. I say to a colleague after they've gone, 'They're not going to buy'.

'How do you know?' my colleague asks.

'I don't know,' I reply. 'I just have a feeling.'

I'm sure you've had the same experience. So learn to accept your instincts. To know what people really want and need, you have to 'tune in' on many levels—to what they're saying, and to what your instincts are telling you.

At some time in the course of business communication, you're going to be in a situation where you have to sell an idea to someone. Or you may be in the awkward situation of having to find a tactful way of telling them that their marvellous idea is not going to work. This really tests your communication skills.

People will not change their opinions just because you tell them they should. 'Look, I know I'm right and this is why. You can see my idea is the only realistic option. Your idea simply won't work.'

What would your reaction be to such statements? People are very predictable in their reactions to challenges like this. If you tell them that their ideas are stupid, they'll feel duty bound to defend them. If you ridicule their position, they have to defend it. Then your task is well-nigh impossible. You're likely to be put in the position of saying, 'Well, this is just how it *has* to be.' That is *not* good communication.

What you must do is present your case so that *the other person accepts it subconsciously*. No idea is ever really accepted or acted upon until the subconscious mind accepts it. You must work with human nature, not against it.

In business communications, as with any transaction between two human beings, you must keep the other person's interests and concerns in mind all the time. Never step on someone's ego: if you do, they will remember it for a long, long time.

Dealing with arguments

If a conversation becomes an argument, what can you do to salvage things? Try these steps:

1 **Let the other person state their case**
  Show that the communication channels are open—you're receiving their message. Don't interrupt. It's even better if you recap their points before you have your turn.

2 **Pause before you answer**
  Don't jump straight in with something like 'I can see your point, but surely you can see …' If you do, you've just undone all the good work of step 1. Stop, nod, and *show* that you're taking on board what was said.

3 **State your case reasonably and accurately**
  Wild accusations and loud voices serve only to alienate people. Studies have shown that others are much more likely to be influenced by a quiet statement of facts, a 'this is why I came to the conclusion I did.'

4 **Let other people support your case**
  This doesn't mean bringing in the cavalry. Two or three people lined up 'on your side' will only make the other person feel more defensive. Others can support your case simply by way of a mention. Or drop supporting facts into the conversation, for example 'I came to this conclusion because xyz happened'. Then it's not just *you* throwing your weight around to get your own way.

5 **Let the other person save face**
  Understand how difficult it is to say you were wrong, or to admit that someone else's idea is better—especially if you've worked on the project for a while.
  Give them an 'out' by saying something like 'Of course, we hadn't got the information about the Jones contract to you before you prepared this, had we?' or 'It's a pity the accounts department has been understaffed this week. How were you supposed to know we had to cut back on X?'

AFTER ONE-ON-ONE COMMUNICATION ...

Can you see how your skills are building up, layer by layer? Once you have a healthy level of self-esteem, everything else follows.

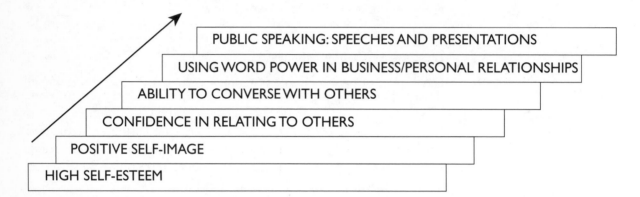

PUBLIC SPEAKING: SPEECHES AND PRESENTATIONS

USING WORD POWER IN BUSINESS/PERSONAL RELATIONSHIPS

ABILITY TO CONVERSE WITH OTHERS

CONFIDENCE IN RELATING TO OTHERS

POSITIVE SELF-IMAGE

HIGH SELF-ESTEEM

It's exciting to see how we can sketch out a blueprint of what we want ourselves and our lives to be like, and work on it level by level until the vision materialises. You go from the first step of taking a good long look at who you *really* are to deciding who you want to be, then work on communicating that vision to your subconscious until it becomes real.

Since you've now mastered the art of conversing naturally and easily with people, let's look at the similarities between casual conversations and public speaking:

Effective conversationalists	Effective public speakers
★ Develop rapport with the listener	★ Develop rapport with the listeners
★ Show an interest in the other person	★ Base speech on audience's knowledge and interests
★ Use eye contact	★ Use eye contact
★ Use pauses for effect	★ Use pauses for effect
★ Keep an eye on the listener's responses and interest level	★ Continually monitor audience response
★ Don't lecture the listener or hog the limelight	★ Don't lecture the audience
★ Use colourful language and anecdotes	★ Use colourful language and anecdotes
★ Act naturally	★ Adopt an easy, natural approach
★ Use interesting words	★ Use interesting words

I could go on, but you get the idea. The most effective speakers are those who speak in a conversational manner. The most unpopular are those who drone on, reading from a long written speech, acting as if they didn't even know they had an audience of live human beings out there. Just as the most unpopular conversationalists are those who treat you as a dummy who'll listen to them without wanting equal time.

What is important in developing good communication skills is *what we say* and *the way we say it*. Positive words and statements help to develop a positive style.

When you're speaking, it sometimes helps to visualise a flow of energy being transmitted between you and the listener. (This works equally well for one-on-one or large audiences.) If it helps, picture two pipelines: one from them to you, the other from you to them.

You *transmit* energy to your listeners via stimulating thoughts and interesting anecdotes. You *take energy from them* if you have them struggling to understand because of obscure terminology, too much information, a monotonous tone or endless stories about yourself. Make it a practice to read the energy level and react accordingly: by cutting out some information, stopping to tell a story to illustrate your point, changing to a chattier style, or simply stopping to listen and draw out the other person.

Communicating effectively involves a change in attitude towards yourself, other people and the language you use.

Think before you speak!

Changing your attitude towards yourself isn't easy, as we've seen. I've already mentioned how lack of academic success contributed to my low self-image. What I haven't mentioned is that as a kid I was also short and fat. At school, I wasn't welcomed as a team player.

'You can be the wicket-keeper,' my school mates would say. 'Even if you can't catch the ball, you're fat enough to stop it.'

My low self-esteem was reinforced by external feedback in those early years. At that age, of course, I had no idea what self-esteem and negative feedback meant. All I knew was that I felt like a loser. But there was still a spark of defiance there. I decided to learn to play the piano, and took up typing and judo. 'I'll show them,' I thought. 'They can't make a fool of me now.'

Nevertheless, that internal programming left scars. As an adult, I would sit at home rather than risk going out alone and being made to look foolish again.

Then a close friend of mine suggested I become involved in public speaking. 'If you can speak so people will listen, you are perceived as an expert,' he told me.

That was over forty years ago. And guess what? The same principles still apply. By learning to speak in public, you give a boost to your self-image. As you develop your skills, you reinforce that image again and again. Increasingly you become a more positive person. When you start to feel secure within yourself, your communication with others automatically improves.

Three years ago, a young person was introduced to me by a mutual friend at a business meeting. During the three-way conversation (which was really a two-way conversation between three people) he just sat there, looking down and not contributing to the proceedings. Ten minutes went by and the meeting ended.

The next day, I phoned him.

'Great meeting you yesterday,' I said. 'Have you got your diary near you?'

'Yes,' he said.

'Can you meet me on Wednesday at 7 p.m.?'

'Yes …?'

'That's great,' I replied. 'I've just enrolled you in an eight-week public speaking course.'

He sounded reluctant. More than reluctant: appalled. Never in my wildest dreams did I think he would turn up—but he did.

Some three years later, guess what he's doing? *Teaching public speaking.* Now this is where the story gets interesting. We were driving to a meeting with a new person in the car. The new person was reserved and withdrawn, just as our hero had been some years earlier. I didn't say anything.

At the end of the evening our hero walked up to me and said, grinning, 'I just told Bob he was doing an eight-week public speaking course!'

Despite the success mentioned above, I'd be leading you down the garden path if I tried to tell you that you'll find giving a speech just as easy as chatting over the fence with your neighbour, or discussing work practices with your colleagues.

But if you approach it systematically, you'll realise that writing and delivering a speech is a straightforward process. You don't have to be a magician. You don't have to be a born speaker, either. If you take it step by step, you'll end up with a good, effective presentation.

It's natural for you to have a few worries, though: the same fears that *everyone* has when they make their first speech. Most of your anxiety is probably based on myths about speaking:

★ Some people are natural speakers.
★ Nerves are uncontrollable.
★ I'll forget what I was going to say!
★ I'll make a fool of myself.

Let's shoot them down before they can do your self-confidence any damage!

1   The natural speaker syndrome

Our attitude towards public speaking is, like so many other things in life, coloured by the events of our childhood. Those events often determine whether we regard public speaking as quite normal and non-threatening, or something to be feared and avoided at all costs.

If your parents were involved in any community groups in which they were accustomed to getting up to speak, then the chances are that you have an open attitude to public speaking.

I know a dynamic young woman who is remarkably poised in any public speaking situation. I asked her about her great self-confidence one day after watching her deal with some particularly probing questions.

'You seem to be able to think on your feet and speak convincingly at the drop of a hat,' I said. 'Have you always been able to do that? Or have you had some training?'

'Thanks for the compliment!' she said. 'No, I haven't had any training.' She thought about it for a few seconds, then shrugged. 'I just seem to have grown up being able to do it. Mum and Dad were always involved with things: business groups, and they were board members of this and that, and Dad was President of Rotary … oh, I don't know. I grew up seeing both of them speaking in public all the time. I just sort of followed in their footsteps, I guess. First the school council, then the debating team … I've never been afraid of speaking in front of people.'

To Olivia, public speaking was just a normal part of life, so *she was never afraid of it.* So simple.

If she had come from a background where her parents *never* spoke in public (other than at family weddings after four neat whiskies) she would probably not have internalised that skill. It's much the same for anyone. If you grew up thinking it wasn't normal to speak in public, you need to change your mental image of what public speaking is.

Once you learn the skills, you'll overcome the fear. You'll realise that the natural-born speaker is a myth.

2   Nerves are uncontrollable

A CB radio can do only one thing at a time: either receive or transmit. The same thing is true when you are the transmitter. If you are pre-occupied with your nervous tension, the nervous impulses take the place of the transmitting impulses.

What you need to remember is this: *you will never lose your nervous tension in any social performance*. Nor would you want to. It's part of your performance. Ask any professional actor or musician.

To combat nervous tension, you must make your nervous system your slave, not your master. To do this you must learn how to *relax*. Relaxation is a most important part of developing effective communication skills.

Try this routine before you speak in public:

★ Visualise the room, the chairs, the platform.
★ Imagine people gradually filling the room and sitting down, then the chairperson calling upon you to speak.
★ Picture yourself slowly walking to the lectern and then standing there looking at the crowd. You are nervous, but controlled.
★ Imagine yourself beginning your speech.
★ If you have put enough detail into this imaginary situation, you should have actually *felt* the natural anxiety attached to the real situation. And if you have controlled yourself in the imaginary situation you are 60 per cent of the way home.

Another effective way to develop self-control in the public speaking situation is through controlled *deep breathing*. Inhale, and count slowly to four. *Think* of the numbers. Actually *see* them in your imagination— 1, 2, 3, 4. Then exhale slowly, thinking, 'I am in control'.

This technique of deep breathing, counting and learning to pause will give you a tremendous feeling of platform control.

Nerves are uncontrollable? Let others think that. *You* can control them just fine.

3   I'll forget the speech

Toastmasters International teaches the following principle:

All speakers have butterflies. Good speakers teach them to fly in formation.

The key is learning how to control your nerves, and you now know how to do that.

If you use notes you will feel more confident. As you become more practised, you will cheerfully do away with your notes. But while you're learning, if you feel more secure holding notes, then do so.

It is easy to psych yourself up to forget. One way of doing this is to try to be word perfect. That was the trouble with *my* very first public speaking performance. I *was* word perfect. So when one word was forgotten, my pattern of thought was disrupted and my whole speech went out the window!

⭐   Don't psych yourself to forget.
⭐   Don't try to be word perfect!

Using notes is fine, but cards are better than loose sheets of paper. Neat, compact notes will allow you to feel confident and relaxed, so that you can think and speak clearly. However, one important piece of advice is to *use notes, not a script!* If you read from a script, you tend to lose spontaneity.

Lots of speakers write and rehearse a script then transfer their notes to cards in point form for the last rehearsal or two and the final performance. Margaret has been a member of Toastmasters for years, so you'd expect that she would be able to speak confidently without notes by now. Mostly she can—but she has a 'trick' to give her a psychological edge. This is what she says:

Once I've blocked out the main ideas, I always write out the speech in full first—it helps me organise my thoughts. Then I change parts when I read it out aloud. Finally, I reduce it to point form on one single sheet or a couple of cards. But when I go up to the lectern, I often take the full speech with me. I've never yet needed to refer to it, but it's like a security blanket. I rarely even look at the cards—but they're there, that's the important part.

4　I'll make a fool of myself

It just isn't sensible for an inexperienced speaker to prepare and present a 20-minute speech to a group of 30 or more people. So if you are a newcomer to public speaking, tread slowly. If you can, plan a first performance of no more than three or four minutes in front of a small group—perhaps give a presentation at work.

Early in your career as a communicator, forget quantity. Go straight for short, high-quality speeches and you will be much less likely to find yourself in an embarrassing situation. And always remain natural.

Now let's look at a step-by-step formula that will help you to produce good, sound speeches. Ready? Let's go.

The five-minute test

For this test, you are going to write a brief talk about the subject you know best: yourself! So get yourself a pen, some plain paper, a few creative thoughts, and five minutes of spare time (not one, not three, but *five* minutes).

Now go—and think before you write.

After you have finished, read your story. Does it go something like this?

> *My name is Elke Bridges, and I live at 10 Smith Street, Dullsville. I am married to Max and we have three children. My occupation is bank teller, and I have been with the bank for the past fifteen years …*

Need we continue? If your story bores you, imagine what it would do to an audience. So, what *should* your story look like if it were to pass the five-minute test?

> *Mr Chairman,*
>
> *If you are anything like me, you find it difficult to remember people's names until you've been introduced a couple of times. So, to make it easy for everyone here to remember me, I'll give you some clues …*

[Turns to whiteboard or flip chart and draws: an 'L', a key, and a bridge.]

My name is Elke Bridges, and over the past fifteen years I have been doing what everyone in this room likes to do—counting money. Mind you, it's not my own, but my job is both interesting and exciting because I am involved with people from all walks of life. Have you guessed it?

I'm a bank teller.

Can you see the difference between the two presentations? One is so standard that it's boring. The other is capable of holding the listeners' interest because it takes *their* point of view into consideration and uses visuals. Even without the visuals, it would have been much more interesting.

It doesn't really matter whether you passed or failed the five-minute test. It's here just to illustrate a point. If you pick up any book on self-improvement you will find that the most important quality you need is *self-confidence*. And self-confidence comes from developing effective communication skills.

But that progression can only occur if you possess the most basic, yet vital requirement.

You have to *want* to improve.

10

A RECIPE FOR SUCCESS: THE SIMPLE INGREDIENTS FOR AN EFFECTIVE SPEECH

You must master a few essential techniques to be an effective speaker. I like to think of them as the ingredients in a successful recipe. Here's the recipe: all you need to know to get started.

As you become more proficient you will probably want to read more about technique. That's good. A number of books will help you do that. But the basic ingredients never change. All you need to do is add a pinch or two of personality and a dash of life experiences, and you will end up with a gourmet meal.

THE RECIPE FOR SPEAKING SUCCESS

Ingredients
- ★ a ripe subject
- ★ a few anecdotes
- ★ a well-rehearsed script
- ★ eye contact
- ★ pause and pace
- ★ empathy
- ★ vocal variety
- ★ facts and/or statistics (to taste)

Method
Pluck one ripe subject from your imagination and allow it to simmer in your mind until ideas begin to rise to the surface. As enthusiasm comes to the boil, skim off ideas and lay aside for a few hours while you prepare facts.

When ideas have matured, mix to a smooth paste with facts and statistics, sprinkle with anecdotes and cook until speech is firm yet light.

To serve

Precede main course with an appetiser consisting of a confident smile and a sparkling introduction. Season main course liberally with eye contact, vocal variety and effective pauses and serve with empathy. Finish with a tasty platter of pertinent points.

It's a recipe that any five-star chef would be proud of. And it'll have your audience licking its lips!

Let's look at the ingredients one by one.

A ripe subject

A green subject is one that you don't know much about. It's young, immature, not fully formed in your mind. You'll feel much more confident if you know and like your subject, and that enthusiasm will come across in your presentation. Later in your speaking career you may be asked to speak on subjects that you need to research in some depth. But when you're starting out it's best to stick to what you know.

Even if you know a lot about your topic, you should still delve deeper. Know what's happening *now* in the field; know it so well that you could talk about it in your sleep. Then all you have to worry about is how you will *present* your speech, not the content.

A few anecdotes

Stories to illustrate your points are the life-blood of your speech. Anecdotes and analogies are the ingredients that make the audience sit up and take notice. When you have decided on your main points, you should think of a short anecdote or analogy to illustrate each one.

Wherever possible, relate your stories to the needs and interests of your audience.

Humorous stories often work well, but there is an art to successful use of humour. If you often have people laughing in conversations, you might have the natural wit's instinct for timing—but don't force it. Even stand-up comedians have problems sometimes.

A well-rehearsed script

There are two steps to confident delivery of a speech: a good script and practice. After you have sorted out your ideas, write your speech and then rehearse it frequently. Each time, change words or sentences that feel awkward, decide where pauses would be effective and practise natural delivery of anecdotes. Rehearse it until you are confident that just a few key words or phrases will be enough to remind you of what you were going to say next.

Then reduce the main points to key words or phrases, and tear up the script. The aim is to talk naturally to the audience, rather than read a speech to them.

By using just a few key words on cards, you are free to concentrate on the audience. You can use eye contact and gestures freely and naturally.

Never attempt to memorise your speech. That's a recipe for disaster. If you forget a line, you could panic and go totally blank.

Eye contact

I can't emphasise enough the importance of eye contact. If you lose eye contact, you lose that vital link between you and the audience.

I have seen speakers who look up at the ceiling so often that I start wondering if their cue cards are stuck to it. Others look at the walls, or stare at their notes—anywhere but the audience!

Sometimes lack of eye contact results from the speaker feeling shy about meeting the gaze of someone in the audience. If this applies to you, stop worrying. You'll find you don't have time to feel embarrassed: you'll be maintaining eye contact for only a second or two before moving onto someone else.

People don't mind you moving your gaze from person to person. They're happy to share you with another human. They're just not willing to share you with the ceiling.

The simple truth is: if you don't make eye contact, people don't feel you are truly communicating with them.

Pause and pace

Experiment for yourself to see how powerful pauses can be. The pause is just as effective in conversations as it is in public speaking. Try this: stop after making an important point. Make eye contact. Signal by using some sort of gesture—a raised hand, for example—that there is more to come. Let the pause stretch out for a moment. Then repeat the point again or come in with the punch line.

You'll be amazed at how quiet your audience becomes. Every eye will be riveted on you. There will be a hush of expectancy. That's because when you pause, the flow of words stops. And when the words stop, the audience automatically looks at you to see what you are going to do or say next. The pause is a powerful signal: *Listen to me!*

You use *pace* in the same way you use the gear shift on your car: you choose the appropriate speed for that moment. Sometimes you want to idle (pause), sometimes cruise slowly, and sometimes accelerate to race away with the audience's emotions.

Using pace doesn't mean you tear along at top speed the whole time. That would serve only to exhaust your audience. They simply won't be able to stay with you. To use pace correctly, you need to monitor your audience constantly to make sure that they're with you and they're entertained.

When you get the opportunity, study other speakers to see how they use pace.

Empathy

Every audience wants to feel that you understand them, that you like them, and that you have prepared this speech just for them.

Find out as much as you can about your audience before you make your presentation. Focus firmly on the background, interests and needs of the people you will have sitting in front of you. When you write anecdotes, make sure they are relevant not only to the theme of your talk but to your listeners.

Vocal variety

It's much more interesting to listen to people if they have an expressive voice. Aim to vary your volume and your pitch.

The easiest way to approach this is to express yourself exactly as you would in any animated conversation. Your voice will naturally rise and fall as you emphasise points of interest or tell a story.

For optimum vocal variety, you can't beat enthusiasm!

Facts and/or statistics (to taste)

Sometimes you will need to include facts or statistics to back up your arguments. The secret is to convert those statistics into mental images for your listeners. Not 10 per cent, but *one person in ten*. Not five out of ten people in the municipality, but *half of your neighbours*. Not X number of years ago, but *about the time when the Beatles were singing 'Lucy in the Sky with Diamonds'*.

See the difference? Mentioning 'neighbours' conjures up immediate mental images; mentioning a song will catapult people back to vivid memories of a certain time or place.

And there you have it. A quick recipe for speaking success. There are more helpful pointers about speech delivery in the next chapter, 'How to Enjoy Presentations'. Meanwhile, let's move on to the actual business of writing a speech.

WRITING A SPEECH

I'm sure the structure of a speech will come as no surprise to you. Ever heard the words *introduction*, *body* and *conclusion* before? I bet they bring back memories of scores of English lessons at high school.

Well, things haven't changed. Whether the words are in an essay or in a speech, your audience needs to 'warm up' to the topic by having an introduction. They need the nitty-gritty information in the body of the work. And they don't want to be dumped unceremoniously at the end without you giving them so much as a goodbye, either.

So follow the simple time-honoured formula—introduction, body and conclusion—to build your speech.

The 'easybuild' technique

Step 1 Brainstorm

Jot down any and every thought that comes to mind about the topic. Put the topic in the middle of the page and write all around it—scraps of sentences, single words, quotations, key words to remind you of supporting anecdotes or jokes.

Step 2 The IBC pages

Take three blank pages. Head them *Introduction*, *Body* and *Conclusion*. Now, after looking at your brainstorming page, jot the ideas down where you think they belong. We're not worrying about form or order at this stage. Be prepared to think about the speech for a few days, and scribble down more ideas as they come. If you've got your speech simmering away in the back of your mind over the course of several days, you'll be surprised at what your subconscious mind will come up with.

Step 3 Write the draft

Let's look at each section of the speech in turn.

The introduction

This is the 'getting to know you' section. It's here that you will establish a relationship with your audience. This is a critical part of your speech. Your listeners will decide, *within the first two minutes*, whether they will tune in to your message or ignore it.

All those listeners out there, with their expectant faces turned to look up at you, are hungry for words they can identify with. They wonder, 'What's in this for me? Is this person going to be interesting or bore us to sobs?'

Here are a few helpful hints:

Do:

★ Be friendly and low-key in your approach.
★ Be easy, confident and positive. *Expect* your audience's attention and you are more likely to get it.
★ Take your time.
★ Make sure that they can hear you and understand you.
★ Use lots of eye contact and pauses to maintain their interest.
★ Make them feel comfortable and relaxed: give them a chance to get to know you.

Don't:

* Antagonise them by coming on too strongly.

* Be negative and show your nervousness. If you don't seem to believe in yourself, your audience certainly won't believe in you.

* Rush through your introduction. If your audience have to struggle to follow your line of thought you will make them feel tense and confused.

Note: the actual preparation of the introduction to your speech should be last. Certainly keep your introduction in mind, and know more or less where you intend to go with it. But don't develop any fixed ideas until *after* you have prepared the body of your speech. Even then don't be surprised if some last-minute changes are necessary to make sure that the tone of your introduction matches the identity of the group you are going to address.

Here is a quick formula to get your introduction underway: the 'ABC' formula.

A is for Attention

* Acknowledge the speaker who introduced you.

* Gain the audience's attention by always speaking from a position where you can be seen and heard.

B is for Break the Ice

* Use pleasant, warm words that allow your personality to shine through, for example 'I'm absolutely delighted to be here—even though I may be shaking in my shoes'.

C is for Communicate

* Many people start a speech by saying, 'I want to talk to you about ...' *Avoid* that approach. Instead, try to *communicate* with a real aim of idea sharing, for example 'My purpose here tonight is to share my ideas with you'.

The body

This part of your speech should be prepared first.

Most newcomers to speaking try to pack too many ideas into their speech. Look for just the best, most important, and most interesting ideas. Wherever possible, look for ways to relate the content to the audience.

The objective of the speech (which is missed by at least half of the people who think they are good speakers) is: *How can I present this subject in a way that will interest the listeners?*

For the sake of argument, let's suppose you are an expert fisherman. You might (God forbid!) tell your audience one of your Big Fish stories, but it's unlikely that it will interest *them*, no matter how memorable it was for *you*.

Do your listeners want to hear about The One That Got Away? It's unlikely.

Would they like to hear about where the big fish are and how *they* can catch them? Much more likely.

The following tips will help you keep your presentation alive:

⋆ **Keep it local**
Make sure your facts are local and uncomplicated.

⋆ **Keep it simple**
No sweeping statements. No overload of information. Don't give your listeners *too much* to think about.

⋆ **Identify**
Use words that identify the audience with your subject—that way you have them hanging on your next sentence. Make them feel that they are part of your subject.

For example, you might want to say that 33.2 per cent of Australians are likely to be divorced at least once. Hmmm. No … that's too complicated. Lots of people won't take in a statistic like that unless it's simplified.

Try rephrasing it this way: 'Five and a half million Australians will be divorced at least once during their lifetime.'

Well, that's better—but let's make it local: 'One person in every three in this room is likely to be divorced at least once in their lifetime.'

Better still. But if you want your audience of forty people to identify with this fact, try this approach: 'Statistically, thirteen people in this room are likely to be divorced at some time in the future.'

Now you are talking to the people in front of you. They are not hearing about anonymous millions outside the room. They are now potential divorcees!

All at once they want to hear what you have to say. This is the way to liven up your speech. Play on the hopes, fears and emotions of your audience, then lead the speech to your theme.

The conclusion

The conclusion should reinforce your ideas and leave listeners with a lasting impression. It must be put clearly and simply. *The last statement you make is likely to be the best remembered.*

Structure your conclusion along these lines:

Tonight I have tried to make you aware of the problem (whatever that might be). I have shown you a solution (if there is one). The decision to move one way or the other rests with you, the people involved. I must make my own decision (pause) … and you must make yours. (STOP!)

Another good idea is to adopt an old journalist's trick: link ideas at the end to ideas at the beginning for a nice circular format. It ties things up neatly.

Avoid using old cliches like:

★ In summing up …
★ And in conclusion …
★ I would just like to add …

and don't ever end with 'Thanking you'!

CHECKLIST FOR SPEECH-BUILDING

1 Open with an easy, warm introduction.
2 Lead slowly and logically into your presentation.
3 Reinforce your views with facts and reasons.
4 Have a definite message and present it clearly.
5 Close with a positive statement.

11

HOW TO ENJOY PRESENTATIONS

Whether the presentations you give are short or long, whether they are given to a few members of staff or a room full of VIPs, you'll find the whole process a lot easier if you *enjoy* it.

And you'll find you will enjoy it, *if you are well-prepared*.

The secret of a smooth presentation lies in knowing your subject matter and presenting it in an entertaining way. For someone like you, who has been so successful in developing powerful people skills, that should be a snap!

To make sure that every presentation you give is a success, however, here are the secrets of a dynamic delivery, drawn from my book, *How to Create and Deliver a Dynamic Presentation* (Simon & Schuster, Australia, 1988). If you want to learn more of the winning elements of super presentations, you might like to read the whole book.

1   ALWAYS SPEAK TO TIME

It doesn't matter whether your presentation is going to be ten minutes or one hour, you *must stay within the time allowed*. How many meetings have you been in where someone waffled about all over the place instead of getting their presentation over and done with? It's frustrating for everyone.

When you start to talk, you will find that it's tempting to wander off the track; to explain just a little bit more; to discuss extra benefits. Resist that temptation. As you take on more speaking tasks, you will find that it is essential to stick to the time available. If you don't, you could extend the meeting or training session unnecessarily—and people won't thank you for that.

If you are not told how long your presentation is to be, ask for guidelines. Then once you have worked out the length of your talk, use these methods to keep track of time:

⋆ Use a watch or clock (be subtle!).
⋆ Have a friend in the audience give you signals.
⋆ Have times for each part of your talk written on the notes—then stick to those times.

2 MAKE SURE YOUR MATERIAL IS SUITED TO THE AUDIENCE

If you are interested in your subject, and knowledgeable about it, then half the battle is won. It has been said that there are no boring subjects, only boring speakers. So, you have to make sure that you have *the right slant* and *the right level*.

You might also like to ask yourself these questions:

⋆ Will they be interested in my subject?
⋆ Can my subject offer them any information they can use?
⋆ Am I the best person for the job?

Find out as much as you can about the audience and their needs, in order to develop rapport during the presentation.

3   KEEP INFORMATION DIGESTIBLE

If you want to keep an audience alert, responsive and on your side, then make it easy for them to remember what you're saying. Limit the amount of information to what is appropriate for the length of your talk and the abilities of your audience. It's better for your audience to remember three facts well than to forget a dozen.

Here are some helpful guidelines:

* Three major items of information in 20 minutes are enough for most people to handle.
* Present your information in bite-size pieces, just enough for your audience to take in one at a time.
* Relate your information to everyday experiences. That will make it easy for your audience to understand its importance, and to remember it.
* Reinforcement is essential. Tell them what you will tell them. Tell them the same thing in a different way. Tell them again, using a parallel.

4   DON'T USE JARGON

Every industry has its own jargon, but unless you are talking to a group from your own industry, don't use jargon.

In fact, if you *really* want to enjoy a presentation, and you want your *audience* to enjoy it, then present technical information in clear, understandable terms. Relate it to their everyday experience. Believe me, being able to speak in this way about technical information is a sought-after talent. You'll have your audience kissing your feet in gratitude.

In other words, *transmit the information on your audience's frequency.*

5   PREPARE THOROUGHLY

Maybe this one should have been listed first. In tandem with a warm, empathetic delivery, it is virtually a guarantee of success.

Dr Ken McFarlane, a brilliant presenter, once commented dryly: 'The truth behind every spectacular presentation is heaps of unspectacular preparation.' Maybe you are one of the very few lucky ones who can walk in unprepared and do well. But if not, then heed Dr McFarlane's advice. Research, plan and draft your material.

How do you go about this?

It's all amazingly straightforward, really:

* Start with a *brainstorm*, a spontaneous ideas session, where you jot down everything that comes into your head to do with the subject.
* *Key word* this material. That is, select a few words which are focus or key words, and then build on them.
* *Reinforce* your key topics with personal stories, analogies, reference to the intended audience's own experiences, and visual aids. (This is essentially what the Apple Tree Approach to session design is all about, explained in detail in *How to Create and Deliver a Dynamic Presentation.*) Personal stories or anecdotes are especially good: you're never stuck for words when you're drawing from your own experience, and people love to listen to a story. You'll enjoy it; they'll enjoy it. Just be careful that you don't get carried away and let a story drag on too long. Short, snappy illustrations are best.

6   PRACTISE YOUR PRESENTATION

Giving a presentation is a skill you can develop. Just like any skill, it needs a *program of practice*.

Consider the case of a fellow called Rick. Rick is an accomplished guitar player and he performs at major concerts all over the country.

Rick signed up for one of my public speaking classes. After the first night, he came up to me and said, 'Doug, I don't get it. Here I am at 27, a guitarist performing in front of up to 5000 people at a time—and doing it well. But tonight, in front of ten people, my nerves are a mess! What gives?'

I started by asking him to calculate how many times he'd practised his guitar playing since he began his career.

'Three times a day, every day for the last ten years, down in the garage,' he replied.

I nodded. 'Every time you get up on stage to play in front of an audience, you're going through a routine that you've practised thousands of times! Now public speaking is just the same. It's a skill which you or I or anyone can learn through practice. If you learn to control your reactions under simulated conditions, you'll have a much better chance of controlling them under real conditions.'

I went on to suggest that he try the three tests which I found so useful when I first started:

★ the *spot* test
★ the *paper* test
★ the *music* test.

The spot test

I call it the spot test because it involves focusing on a spot on the wall as you rehearse your talk.

Here's what to do. In your imagination, set the scene for your speech—the hall, the audience, the time and so on. Then visualise the lead up to your talk—the introduction. Then stand up and start. 'Good evening/afternoon. I'm glad to be here to talk about …'—and say it with conviction, as if it really was the big event.

As you go through your speech, focus on a spot on the wall. The reason for this is that if you can't do it in front of a blank wall, you won't be able to talk in front of people.

Feel self-conscious? Don't worry. All the best public speakers—as well as actors, politicians and performers of any sort—have done it at some stage. And who's going to know, anyway?

You might still be wondering whether talking to a blank spot is really going to do you any good. After all, it doesn't seem to have much to do with relating to a real audience.

Let me tell you about an experiment at the University of Illinois, one which has been quoted many times in different sources. A number of student basketballers were divided into three groups and tested for their ability to score baskets. Their scores were carefully recorded. Then, the three groups were given different sets of instructions.

Group One were told to come into the gym every day to practise shooting.

Group Two were told to do no practice at all.

Group Three were told to practise—but in a very different way! 'Don't report to the gym,' they were told, 'but every night in the dorm, imagine yourselves at the gym practising.'

For half an hour every day, Group 3 'saw' themselves throwing the ball and scoring baskets and improving dramatically. They continued this 'inner practice' every day.

After a month, the three groups were tested again. These were the results:

* Group One (who practised shooting every day) showed a 26 per cent improvement in their scores.
* Group Two (who didn't practise at all) showed no improvement.
* Group Three (who had practised only in their minds) improved as much as Group One!

Still think that talking to blank wall while imagining the audience won't have any effect?

The paper test

This activity trains you in keeping your feet still when you speak. You'll avoid the habit of rocking, rolling and shuffling—and therefore distracting your audience from your message.

Place a piece of ordinary white paper on the floor. Stand on it, and then draw around your shoes with a felt-tip pen—and that's where your feet stay as you speak.

Now go through the spot test again, keeping your feet under control as you speak.

The music test

Our guitarist, Rick, thought he'd like this one!

At a speaking engagement there are many distractions: noises from outside, people coming and going. Once you allow yourself to be distracted, you lose your train of thought. To prevent this, try the music test.

Put on some music with the volume set at just above a comfortable listening level. Start your talk with the music playing, focusing on the spot and keeping your feet still.

At first you'll find it almost impossible to maintain your line of thought. But you'll get better at it, and you'll be able to concentrate on what counts—getting your message across in a fun and exciting way.

Rick could see the sense in these suggestions. He headed off for his first practice session in his garage.

So how about it? Find your own garage and put in some practice, controlling your reactions under simulated conditions.

7 MAKE SURE THE AUDIENCE IS NOT DISTRACTED BY VISUALS, VERBALS OR VOCALS

There are three aspects of presentation which influence the effectiveness of your communication:

★ the *visual* aspect—what they see you do
★ the *verbal* aspect—what they hear you say
★ the *vocal* aspect—how they hear you say it.

All of these work together to make your message clear and interesting.

The most powerful effect is visual—facial expressions, gestures, body stance. If there is any competition among the three, the visual will predominate.

Learn to control any distracting habits you may have which affect the visual, verbal and vocal aspects of your presentation. Ask a friend to tell you of any distracting habits you display while speaking—such as standing on one foot, scratching your nose, tugging at your ear, using *um*, *ah*, *sort of* and *you know*, or using a slurred, an unclear or a monotonous way of speaking.

Using an audio or video recorder will help you to analyse your voice or picture.

Pinpoint any problems and then eliminate them so that the visual, verbal and vocal aspects of your presentation reinforce each other.

8 DELIVER YOUR MESSAGE AT AN APPROPRIATE PACE

Naturally, you want your personality to come across in your delivery.

The main problem usually is that people speak too quickly. Nervous, they want to get the message across as quickly as possible.

Is that what you do when you're speaking to friends? No. You speak naturally, at an appropriate pace for the material—probably without even having to give it a second thought.

So relax. Remember, your audience needs time to take in what you are saying. If you speak more quickly than they can take it in, your message is lost.

Delivering an effective speech can be likened to driving a car—you need to speed up and slow down now and again, but mostly you move along at a steady pace.

To reinforce your message, however, you need to vary the pace.

Here are some things you can try:

* Practise with a metronome. The regular beat will help you to pace your delivery.
* Use a cassette recorder to check your rate.
* Use the pause for effect, and wait for the laughter, noise etc. to die down.
* Observe the audience as you speak and adjust your pace to maximise the effect on them.

9 MAINTAIN EYE CONTACT

When you're having a conversation with another person, you look them directly in the eye. That way the other person knows you're talking to them and maintains a direct, open contact.

It's the same with public speaking. If you establish eye contact with the individual members of the audience, they will be drawn into your talk. They will feel that you are speaking directly to each of them.

If you're using notes, pause each time you refer to them, then re-establish eye contact and continue your talk. Practise in front of a mirror; or better still, have a friend monitor your eye contact during your speech.

If you look at the audience, they will keep listening.

10   BE ENTHUSIASTIC

There's no doubt about it, we all enjoy any activity more if we're enthusiastic about it. And your audience will certainly enjoy it more if your enthusiasm comes across.

Never forget, when you're speaking in front of a group of people, you're a salesperson for your own ideas. A performer, presenting a show.

You're projecting your personality.

If you're enthusiastic about a subject in which you have a genuine interest, it will come across in your talk. The audience will be convinced that you believe that your subject is interesting and important. *They'll buy your ideas.*

Here are a few tips to demonstrate your enthusiasm:

⭐ Don't hide behind the lectern. Let yourself be seen.

⭐ Start off on a lively and encouraging note with something like, 'I'm delighted to be here tonight to share my ideas with you.'

⭐ Keep up the pace, especially at the beginning of your talk when judgements are being formed about you.

⭐ Employ all of your presentation skills to convey your enthusiasm: an expressive voice, appropriate gestures and emphasis, and humour.

Use the full force of your personality to project your enthusiasm for the subject!

CHECKLIST FOR ENJOYING PRESENTATIONS

1   Always speak to time.
2   Make sure your material is suited to the audience.
3   Keep information digestible.
4   Don't use jargon.
5   Prepare thoroughly.
6   Practise your presentation.
7   Make sure the audience is not distracted by visuals, verbals or vocals.
8   Deliver your message at an appropriate pace.
9   Maintain eye contact.
10   Be enthusiastic.

12

SPEAKING FOR THE FUN OF IT

Something entirely unexpected could happen once you start speaking in public.

You might actually find you enjoy it! If so, you're likely to look for more speaking opportunities.

There are lots of ways you can speak purely for the fun of it. Here are a few ideas:

★ **Volunteer to give entertaining speeches at weddings and other family celebrations**
Let's face it, most speeches on family occasions are pretty awful. Why not give everyone a treat with an amusing, well-planned speech?

★ **Contact local clubs and offer to be a guest speaker**
Clubs such as Rotary, View, Apex, Salespeople with a Purpose and many more are all keen to book talented speakers to entertain their members. Offer to speak on your area of interest or expertise.

* **Join a speaker's club**
  Clubs like Toastmasters International and International Training in Communication are great places to hone your skills and have fun at the same time. You get practice in writing and delivering speeches as well as opportunities to practise speaking off the cuff. You also have the opportunity to pit yourself against other talented speakers in competitions.

* **Offer to be the media relations officer at your place of work**
  This will give you many more opportunities to speak to newspaper, television and radio reporters. Writing articles and press releases is also good practice for getting across essential points in speech writing.

* **Ask for training responsibilities at work**
  By training groups of various sizes, you will not only gain confidence, but you will have the opportunity to try out a whole lot of different presentation techniques.

SPEECHES AT SHORT NOTICE

You won't always have weeks to prepare your speeches. People have a habit of asking good speakers to step in at the last moment.

Here are some handy shortcuts for those occasions when you have to come up with a speech at short notice:

1 Past, present and future

Relate today's world, or event, to the past and future for quick ideas. What kind of people are going to be in your audience? Where do they work? Are they facing any particular problems at this particular time?

Think about their position in comparison with past workers. Are things better? Worse? Can you think of any inspirational leaders from the past that this audience could relate to? Can you speak to one or two people who will be in the audience and ask them for amusing anecdotes from the past?

What about the future? Does it look promising? (If it doesn't, don't say much about it in your talk. Any audience would rather go away feeling uplifted than depressed!) If the future looks bleak, then concentrate on the positive qualities of the people in front of you and their achievements in the past.

2   Who, what, why, when, how and if

Virtually anyone can come up with a speech by working through the old friends: who, what, why, when, how and if.

Who would inspire this audience? Who is responsible for setting up the company? Who could provide the basis of an inspiring or amusing anecdote? Who is in the audience?

What brought you here today? What is important to the audience in front of you? What is the common link between you and them? What can you say to inspire, entertain or help them? What is happening in the world that relates to them?

Why are they here today? Why did someone first decide to come up with the product or service they provide? Why are they important to the community?

When did the company or firm come into being? When did you decide to do whatever you're now involved in? Is there anything from your past, from your personal story, that can inspire these people? When was the first conference of this type held?

How can you best explain a new concept or idea to your audience? How can you help them in their business or in their daily lives? How can they make life better for themselves or for others? How can they make more money, make better use of time, gain publicity for their business, find more customers? Asking 'how' can generate enough material for a dozen speeches.

If (or *what if*): *What if* the people in your audience started putting your ideas into practice tomorrow? How would it change things for them? What if they set different goals, decided to set about meeting different people? What if they all decided to aim for 10 per cent more efficiency? What if they all resolved to help someone in some way every day?

The sample questions under each of these headings are just a few of the many, many questions you could generate by asking who, what, why, when, how and what if? This is a useful technique at any time, but *particularly* when you don't have much time to prepare.

The information in Part III should have not only removed some of the fear of public speaking, but shown you that it might actually be something you could do simply for the fun of it!

PART IV

WRITTEN COMMUNICATION

13

WRITING WELL ... WRITING NATURALLY

It doesn't make much sense to work on improving every other aspect of your life if you forget about (or ignore) developing your written communication skills.

Some of us have little or no need to put things in writing, or we employ someone else to do it for us. Many, however, frequently need to write to others or follow up meetings, speeches and presentations with printed material or a report. If you do this, you'd better know how to do it properly, or you can sabotage all the hard work you've put in at making a good impression.

If you have given speeches, you're already well on the way to knowing what constitutes a natural, easy style that will serve you well in all forms of communication. In writing speeches, you get to know which words work well in getting the message across. You learn that jargon and archaic language don't work. You learn that long, complicated sentences don't work. You learn that people prefer a warm, personal approach.

The same standards apply to *everything* you have to write. Whether you are writing business letters, social letters, reports, articles or books, you should aim at developing a friendly style that feels natural to write.

Natural does not mean sloppy or careless. The hasty letter you dash off to a friend or your mother can be full of sentences like, 'You'll never guess where I went on Saturday!!! Marcie's house, you know the one she bought on the lake? Nr. Port Macquarie? Well, wait til I tell you ...' etc. Rows of exclamation marks and abbreviated sentences probably sound delightfully 'you' to the recipient, but that's a bit too casual for most purposes.

Being too casual is not the problem for another class of writers. I'm talking about the people who are left with hangovers from their school essay-writing days. Put a pen in their hands, and they undergo some sort of transformation. Even letters to friends are formal, with beautifully executed sentences and flowery words. They sound pompous, pretentious and, most of all, dull.

This, of course, is not the way they mean to come across. They're trying desperately hard to write well. So why doesn't it work?

For many reasons. Here are some:

★ They know that the written word is more permanent. Oral communication is over in a short time. Unless your words have been recorded, only the memory remains. But with writing—well, all sorts of dreaded things can happen with our writing. People might show it to someone else. They might talk among themselves about how poor our grammar or spelling or sentence structure is. Writing can be kept for weeks or months or years. Knowing this makes people try too hard to be formal or correct.

★ Writing is seen as 'difficult'. 'I know what I want to say, but it's so hard to put it in writing' is a common complaint. People run into strife with anything from writing a clear sentence to structuring sections of a report so that people can follow it easily.

★ Writing takes so long to do properly. We all know what it's like to labour over writing something for hours, only to read it through and know (with that awful sinking feeling) that it still needs lots of work. Any one of these things is likely to happen:

 – You shove it into a folder 'to do later'—and never finish it.
 – You delegate the job to someone else to finish (someone who often doesn't know enough about it to finish the piece properly, or resents the extra work).
 – You make a few haphazard changes, then think, 'That'll *have* to do!', and send it on its way—to create a poor impression at the other end.

Writing well doesn't have to be such a tortured process. There a few simple rules of style and structure which will suit a variety of writing needs.

SIMPLE RULES FOR WRITING

1   Know your audience

As well as knowing what you want to say, you must know to whom you want to say it. That doesn't mean just 'Oh, it's to Jenny Bloggs down at Wonderful Widgets'. Who is Jenny Bloggs? Does she feel more comfortable with a formal or informal style? What are *her* letters like? Is she a close friend or a stranger? What is her level of literacy likely to be?

In the same way that you will adjust a speech to the type of audience, you can choose from a variety of writing styles to suit the recipient. Although you must always try to sound like yourself, you will be able to adjust the tone of your letter, report or instructions to suit the audience.

For instance, a psychologist writing for a professional journal has a fairly easy task, since most of the audience could be presumed to be professionals also, and would have no difficulty understanding any technical language or the concepts used. If, however, the same psychologist were faced with the task of explaining a case to a general audience, the task would be more difficult: it is necessary to make sure both the message and the language are readily understood.

2   Know what you want to say about your subject

You may know generally what you want to write about, but do you know how you are going to express it in writing? You will find that you tend to waffle unless you jot down the main points you want to make.

3   Know how you're going to say it

Are you going to:

* explain?
* compare and contrast two ways of doing something?
* summarise?
* analyse?
* describe?
* plead?
* argue?

You may find that more than one of these approaches will suit your needs in the same piece of writing. Just remember: if you are making a complaint, be tactful and reasonable. Where possible, offer the other person a chance to save face and/or make things right.

If you are explaining, stick to *simple sentences and words*. Simple does not mean babyish. Good writing is clear and direct, but technical expressions and words are used where necessary to preserve the correct meaning.

4 Keep related points together

Some writers run into difficulties when they fail to plan their work. They reread their drafts, and discover that they somehow have managed to keep repeating themselves and making points in a haphazard way all over the place.

How can you avoid this? Firstly, by planning: decide on the main points you want to make. Secondly, by writing a paragraph to explain each point. The first sentence should state the main idea. The rest of the paragraph should support it. If you have a related issue that needs to be mentioned, write another paragraph and then *keep related points together*. You can link the two paragraphs by using a sentence beginning with such phrases as: 'A related issue is …' or 'Furthermore, …'

5 Write in plain English

People won't thank you for making them consult a dictionary to find out what on earth you are going on about. In fact, they're not even likely to look up a dictionary at all. They'll toss aside your note or report or letter in irritation and go back to it later—maybe. You make no friends by using pompous, outdated or archaic language. You may even make enemies, if people feel you are in some way placing yourself above them.

In most cases, it is better to use a relaxed, casual style: just a little more formal than speech, but enough to convey the impression to people that you are speaking to them personally.

6 Don't use words you don't understand

If you're not sure of the meaning of a word, don't use it! If people realise your words are inaccurate or inappropriate, they are likely to believe the same of your work. Some commonly confused words are:

* affect and effect
* compose and comprise
* compliment and complement; complimentary and complementary
* adverse and averse
* phase and faze.

7   Avoid the use of jargon or 'in' words

We have all had the experience of being irritated by the use of jargon (the technical language of a profession or trade) when we don't know enough about the subject to understand the meaning of the words. For instance: if you were studying linguistics you would know about *neurological impress and morphology*; if you were familiar with computers you would know the difference between *ROM and RAM, CPUs and co-processors*; if you had studied psychology you would understand *Gestalt principles, empiricism and psychosocial stages*. If you *didn't* understand these concepts, however, and someone presented you with reading material which assumed you *did*, you would be likely to feel annoyed or threatened or both. If you have to write something containing technical language for non-technical people, make sure you include explanations of potentially unfamiliar terms.

Similarly, avoid use of 'in' words (or vogue words) such as *paradigm, interface, parameters, dichotomy* and so on. Even people who have heard them before sometimes have to look them up to remember what they mean.

In short: you should always write as clearly and convincingly as possible. Don't worry about trying to impress people. You will do that automatically if you simply make an honest effort to get your message across in a way that makes it easy for the reader.

USING THE RULES IN A VARIETY OF SITUATIONS

Social

People place great store by small expressions of good manners. If you stay with someone for a period of time, if they take you out on the town, if you attend a dinner or a party, always write and thank your hosts.

Do not type a thank-you note or ask your secretary to do it for you. A personal note is better than a card. Or, if you do buy a card, make sure you write a paragraph or two inside it. Mention the main course, or the scenery, or the play, or the stimulating company and say how much you enjoyed it—make it personal. And write it by hand.

Business

A business communication will necessarily be more formal than a handwritten thank-you note, but care is just as essential. You can ruin everything you've done to present a positive image and a professional attitude if your subsequent written communication is:

★ poorly expressed
★ pretentious
★ ungrammatical
★ badly spelt.

IF YOU CAN'T WRITE

If you can't write effectively, you have the following choices:

★ Read books or take courses to find out how to write.
★ Hire people who can write.

Read books or take courses

Many books are available to help you improve your writing skills. You can start off at as basic a level as you wish by going into a bookstore and asking for a fourth- or fifth-grade English school workbook, and working your way up. Or you can ask at a local TAFE about courses to brush up on basic English writing skills.

If you think the basics are all right, but you need to work on the finer points of structure and grammar, there are excellent books around on effective business writing or the basics of good style. Look in the business or communication section of any good bookstore. Here are just a few titles:

Style Manual for Authors, Editors and Printers, 5th edn, Australian Government Printing Service, Canberra, 1994.

Piotrowski, Maryann, *Effective Business Writing*, Harper & Row, New York, 1989.

Renton, N. E., *Renton's Elements of Style and Good Writing*, Schwartz & Wilkinson, Information Australia, Melbourne, 1990.

Strunk, William Jr & White, E. B., *The Elements of Style*, Macmillan, New York, reprinted annually.

Zinsser, William, *On Writing Well*, Harper & Row, New York, 1988.

Hire other people who can write

'Other people' may be anyone from a staff member to a freelance writer. If you are in the position of hiring staff, look for someone who enjoys writing and has obtained good marks in English and spelling at school. If the ability to write well is particularly important in the staff you hire, narrow down the applicants to a short list and give them all some specific writing tasks to do after the interview.

If you simply need someone from time to time who can turn out a good report, article or training notes for you, look for a freelance writer or a ghost writer. A ghost writer is someone who takes your ideas or rough copy and translates them into effectively written material. The material appears under your name.

Where do you find a writer? Try looking up writers' organisations in the yellow pages, then phone and ask them to recommend someone. Some writers advertise their services, in the 'work wanted' columns of newspapers. Others list with community service agencies. Another source is the staff of a local newspaper or magazine.

If you do find someone, ask to see samples of published work, if possible, to see if their style seems to suit your needs. They too can be asked to write some sample pieces for you.

Even if you hire other people to do most of your writing for you, it's worthwhile to try to improve your own skills as much as you can. Inevitably, you'll need to dash off something quickly one day when there's no one else at hand to do it for you. If you've gone to a lot of trouble to build up your self-image and speaking skills, why not add the finishing touches and work on your writing as well?

A writer's troubleshooting guide

The problem	The solution
I can't get started.	Brainstorm: jot down ideas.
I can't get organised.	Rank your points in order of importance.
It's too much work.	1 Approach in bite-size chunks: brainstorm and plan in one session; begin writing in another. Do a section at a time, edit the draft, then polish. 2 Get help or share the task.
I don't sound like myself (too pompous/ too formal).	Explain it as you would to someone in a conversation; write it the same way, then edit and polish.
My grammar/spelling/sentence structure is faulty.	Buy workbooks to help you at an appropriate level; enquire at a TAFE about appropriate courses; get private tuition; *practise*.
My writing doesn't seem to 'flow'.	You need help with your writing style. Buy books on effective writing; study the structure of magazine or newspaper articles. (Copying these articles will teach you a lot about structure and style.)
I don't have time to spend on writing.	Hire extra staff; hire a professional writer; look at your management of time and prioritise tasks differently if necessary.
I take too long over even the simplest writing task.	Plan your writing better. Try setting limits: 30 minutes or an hour to accomplish one definite part (or the entire piece, if it's short).
I simply hate to write.	Do it early in the day when you're fresh; set time limits then reward yourself with a more pleasurable activity. When you write something that works well, take a minute to feel pleasure at a job well done—then try to recall that feeling when it's time to start the next task.
I have trouble writing in simple terms when I'm trying to explain something technical to someone who isn't familiar with the jargon.	Pretend you have to explain it to a 12-year-old; clarify the terms as you go. To practise clear, step-by-step writing, try this: Write down the steps in using a common household appliance (e.g. a blender or a microwave oven) for someone who has never seen or used it before. Make sure you don't leave out a step. Or try describing the steps in doing something— baking a cake, making a bookcase, driving a car.

WRITING THAT WORKS

So far we've dealt with the basics that apply to any kind of writing:

1 Know your audience.
2 Know what you want to say about your subject.
3 Know how you're going to say it.
4 Keep related points together.
5 Write in plain English.
6 Don't use words you don't understand.
7 Avoid the use of jargon or 'in' words.

These simple rules will help you get your message across to most people. But now, let's look at a range of communications you might need to attempt, from letters to newspaper advice columns.

The main thing to remember is to inject your personality into your writing. (Telemarketers are often instructed to smile as they introduce themselves, because people on the other end of the phone really *can* tell the difference. Similarly, a friendly and confident approach comes through in your writing.)

Two things you need to remember:

★ Always keep the reader's needs in mind
★ Let your personality come through.

The instruction to 'let your personality come through' does *not* mean you should adopt a flippant style. Simply let your reader feel that a warm, caring human being wrote the words they are reading. Far too many letters, reports and instructions give the impression that they were thought up and written solely by a computer.

LETTERS

You will probably have to write a lot of letters in your lifetime, ranging from personal letters to friends and family, to more formal letters connected with your job.

I did not say *formal* letters. I said *more formal*. There is a difference. Formal can sound like a stuffed shirt. Formal may be cold and uncaring or riddled with jargon. Formal letters may even irritate people to the extent that they are moved to take a course of action that is the exact opposite of what you wanted.

However, if you follow the number one rule—*keep the reader's needs in mind*—it's much easier to sit down and write any kind of letter. This is so whether you are writing to persuade, to congratulate, to inform, to remind or even to request payment. Let's look at a couple of examples to see what a difference it makes when you write with a *real* person in mind.

A letter requesting payment

You should aim not only to collect the payment owing, but also to give the reader an opportunity to save face.

Not this:

> *Dear Ms Smith*
>
> *Payment of your account with XYZ Company is now 40 days past due. As our terms require payment within 21 days, we request that payment be made immediately.*
>
> *We would appreciate your cheque in payment of the outstanding amount of $457.50 within three days of the date of this letter.*
>
> *Please contact us immediately if there is a problem with payment.*

But this:

> *Dear Ms Smith*
>
> *At XYZ Company, we pride ourselves on the quick and efficient service we offer our customers. To maintain our high standards, we rely on the cooperation of good customers like yourself in prompt settlement of accounts.*
>
> *It's very easy to overlook payment, and we are sure you will not mind this reminder. Our records show the amount outstanding on your account is $457.50.*
>
> *If for some reason you are unable to act now, we'll be happy to work with you to find a solution. Just give us a call.*

A letter to inform and persuade

The following letters were designed to impart information and to persuade prospective clients to attend a free workshop. The first gives all the necessary information, but gives no hint that the writer has a personality. The second is designed to sound more like someone talking to the reader.

Not this:

Dear Ms Smith

Our company, XYZ Accounting, is currently planning a series of workshops on How to Manage Your Finances.

We would like to invite you and a partner to attend one of these workshops on any of the following dates: 3, 10, 17 or 24 August. Each workshop will run from 7.00 p.m. to 9.00 p.m. These workshops have been very popular with attendees in the past, and we anticipate a positive response. As we have to limit places to 40 participants, we recommend you contact us soon to secure your place.

If you wish to take advantage of this offer, you should notify Ms Jones on 9731 2679 as soon as possible in order that we may send you a formal invitation.

But this:

Dear Ms Smith

At last! A chance to learn how to really make your money work for you, in our popular How to Manage Your Finances. In this fast-paced two-hour workshop, you will find out exactly how to get ahead in life. And all for free!

We take pleasure in inviting you and a partner to the session that suits you best: 3, 10, 17 or 24 August. Each session runs from 7.00 p.m. to 9.00 p.m.

Our workshops are fun, easy to follow and packed full of good ideas and practical advice. There's just one problem—they are so popular that places (limited to 40 per session) fill up very quickly!

So, if you'd like to come, phone Liz Jones here at XYZ Accounting right away. Liz will be happy to send you a formal invitation—for an evening that could change your life! We look forward to seeing you.

Hint #1

To help you use language that appeals to most readers, be on the look-out for books on copywriting and advertising. You'll discover words which will help you to persuade people or sell a service. Such books are useful, as long as you don't lose sight of the fact that readers are human beings with likes, dislikes, needs and worries just like you! Don't talk down to them and *never* think in terms of manipulating them.

Hint #2

We all get countless letters through the mail, from official letters and bills to junk mail. From now on, when you spot a letter with an appealing style, *save it*.

Gradually build up your own library of letters designed for all sorts of audiences and purposes. As you are saving letters that appeal to you, they probably match your personal style and will therefore be easy to adapt to your needs.

PRESS RELEASES

Many people look upon press releases as simply factual statements to the media. They don't bother taking too much time over them. The writer often assumes that 'they' will fix anything that needs fixing at the other end.

'They'—the media people concerned—are more likely to file them in the bin. They're busy people. If you don't care enough to take time with your writing, they sure won't. Unless it's a very slow news day.

A press release is indeed a statement of information. But it also has another job to do: to *sell* you or your products. You need to use elements of persuasive writing.

Here's a simple guide to writing an effective press release:

1   Submit your information on an appropriately headed press release form.
2   Select and organise your information before you start writing. In general, a press release should deal with only one item of information.

3   Think of an interesting headline that tells the reader what the press release is about.
For instance:
Joe Bloggs honoured with prestigious award
or
XYZ Accounting seminars a sell-out

4   In the first paragraph, sum up the information you are providing. (Many newspaper articles do this in the first paragraph. Look for examples.)
For instance:
Joe Bloggs, General Sales Manager of Supa Cereals, is the first Australian ever to be awarded the prestigious Pan-Pacific Sales Trophy. At a ceremony in the ballroom at the Sydney Casa Blanca Hotel on Tuesday, 10 August, Mr Bloggs passed on the secrets of his success to a capacity audience.

5   Outline your news in clear, reader-friendly terms. It is best to put only one piece of information in each paragraph. If you are writing a press release about an event, you should include:

★   nature and name of the event

★   name of person(s) present

★   when it happened

★   where it happened

★   why the event is noteworthy

★   what will happen or is expected to happen as a result of the event.

If you are writing a press release about a product, you should include:

★   name of the product

★   what it does/is used for

★   any special features; technical details

★   why it is better than similar products

★   who should use it

★   details of price, delivery and supply.

6   Finish with a contact name and number: 'For more information contact Jane Smith on 9233 1987.'

7   Check that the length does not exceed two pages—a single page is best.

ARTICLES AND NEWSPAPER COLUMNS

Writing articles or columns for newspapers can help you in three ways:

1 You become a recognised 'expert' (people generally assume some-one who is published is worth listening to).
2 You offer many, many more people the benefit of your experience, ideas and expertise.
3 You express your personality in a way that attracts opportunities and/or customers.

How do you start?

Well, first of all, check that you have something useful to say. If you have, the next thing to decide is whether you're going to write the material yourself or have a professional writer do it for you.

There are thousands of people out there with great ideas, but only a fraction of them make it into print—because writing is 'too hard'.

The clever ones don't let their lack of expertise stop them. They subcontract the work to people who *can* write. After all, why should perfectly good ideas and useful advice go to waste simply because you haven't yet learnt to write like a professional?

This attitude is sensible. If you have a message that will benefit others, it doesn't make sense to keep the lid on it until you have the time to learn to write. People hire professionals to paint their houses, plumbers to fix their pipes, and graphic designers to design their logos. They don't assume they can do the job simply because they can hold a paintbrush or draw a line. They call in an expert to do it for them. Hiring a writer to convey a message in a professional manner makes just as much sense.

If you *do* decide to hire a ghost writer or an editing consultant, you will need to provide the following information:

1 the needs and interests of your intended audience
2 the main points you want to make
3 the *slant* you want to take (a new or different approach to the topic)
4 details of any anecdotes which could illustrate your points.

You can do one of the following:

* Write the article in its entirety before giving it to a ghost writer to edit or rewrite.
* Hand a ghost writer an outline or a rough copy to turn into an article.
* Discuss your needs with your writing consultant as they record your instructions on tape.

Writing your own copy

You may, however, prefer to write your own copy. If that is so, make sure you read what others have written. You may think this sounds a bit like my earlier advice about collecting suitable letters written by other people, and you are right. You can learn a lot by analysing the work of others.

Don't just read the work of people in your own field (for example, finance, real estate, marketing). You will get many more useful ideas if you broaden your horizons.

Articles

Study the *style* of articles as well as their structure. Most well-written articles have the following features in common:

* They are written in a clear, simple style.
* They use a 'hook' to draw the reader into the story: a quote, an anecdote, a startling statement.
* They cover three to five main points only. Any more may result in information overload. (The exception here is the 'list' article: 'Ten Ideas to Prevent Overload'; 'Sales Tips for Each Month of the Year', etc.)
* They reinforce their message with anecdotes which help readers create a picture in their minds.
* They are neatly rounded off, with a satisfying conclusion.

Advice columns

Writing a column allows you to be a bit more idiosyncratic. This is a real opportunity to let your personality shine through. Regular readers feel they 'know' you through your writing style. (Even if you use a ghost writer, a good one should be able to write with your 'voice'.)

You can be chatty, humorous, helpful, informative—whatever suits your personal style and gets your message across to the reader.

If you see a need for a column in your area of expertise in a local newspaper (or in an industry newsletter), consider pitching your idea to the editor. Explain the benefits to readers and offer to provide a couple of sample columns to help the editor make a decision. Just make sure you can commit yourself to at least six months' worth of columns.

The experience will be invaluable. You will also gain enhanced credibility and visibility—and, of course, increased self-confidence!

Writing skills are a vital part of the total communication package. Learn to master the basics, then seek out opportunities to present your ideas in print.

PART V

PUTTING IT ALL TOGETHER

14

SHOW PEOPLE WHO YOU ARE ...

Everything in this book has been designed to show you how you can, step by step:

★ develop self-esteem
★ develop and project a positive self-image
★ become a confident speaker
★ express yourself effectively in writing.

In short, it shows you how to develop powerful people skills by becoming an effective communicator. All communication (non-verbal, verbal and written) links together to *show people who you are*.
   You can change:

★ your self-image
★ the way people feel about you
★ the way you talk
★ the way you listen
★ the way you behave

while still keeping the essential core of personality that is you.
   Each improvement you make in any one area will have an immediate effect on your self-esteem and your self-image—and will therefore impact on every other area. Work on yourself not only for the benefits you'll see in your life and relationships, but most importantly to gain a sense of fulfilment. When you take the time to think about what is important to you, then (1) learn how to translate that into action and (2) learn how to communicate it to others, you will feel much more contented with your life.

THE STEPP METHOD

The most practical way to reach your ultimate goal, powerful skills in human interaction, is to (1) identify your major goal and (2) then work *backwards* to establish what each step will be.

I call this approach (logically enough) the STEPP method— Strategies To Expand People Power.

Think of your strategies to expand your people power as points on a staircase, with your goal at the top. By approaching your goal in a series of logical steps, you make your task much simpler and much more achievable.

It's like identifying two possible ways to climb a mountain. One is rough, uncharted territory with hazards at every step—and you never know what unwelcome surprise might await you behind each rocky outcrop. The other is a carefully marked path, with rest stops and handrails to assist your progress. Doesn't it make more sense to choose the path that is guaranteed to get you there safely?

Let's assume that your ultimate goal is to have warm, empathetic communication skills: 'people skills' that will stand you in good stead for happiness and success in your personal and professional life. 'Powerful people skills', then, is the goal that goes on the top of your staircase. Along with it will go your plan for an ongoing study program for continual improvement.

From there you work backwards. Maybe the biggest achievement you can imagine before getting to your goal is being able to confidently deliver a speech to a large audience. So that goes in second from the top.

What else logically leads up to that? Perhaps it's being able to plan, write, practise and effectively deliver a speech to a small group. And so on and so on and so on …

What follows is a fairly typical example of the steps required by an average person on their way to being a confident, successful person who is able to hold their own in large and small groups.

Some of your steps may be different, depending upon your own particular strengths and weaknesses identified in the early chapters. You can, however, use this example as a model.

Goal: To possess powerful people skills and to plan an ongoing self-study program for continual improvement

Identify new goals

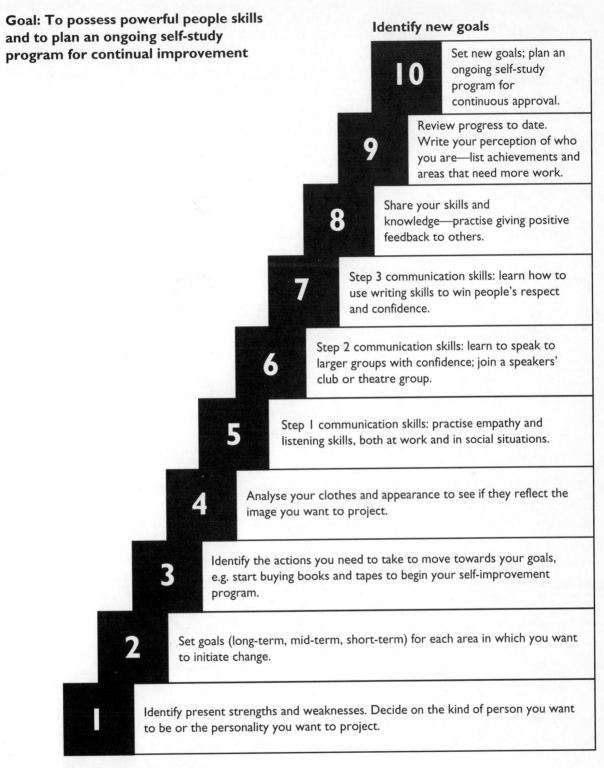

10 Set new goals; plan an ongoing self-study program for continuous approval.

9 Review progress to date. Write your perception of who you are—list achievements and areas that need more work.

8 Share your skills and knowledge—practise giving positive feedback to others.

7 Step 3 communication skills: learn how to use writing skills to win people's respect and confidence.

6 Step 2 communication skills: learn to speak to larger groups with confidence; join a speakers' club or theatre group.

5 Step 1 communication skills: practise empathy and listening skills, both at work and in social situations.

4 Analyse your clothes and appearance to see if they reflect the image you want to project.

3 Identify the actions you need to take to move towards your goals, e.g. start buying books and tapes to begin your self-improvement program.

2 Set goals (long-term, mid-term, short-term) for each area in which you want to initiate change.

1 Identify present strengths and weaknesses. Decide on the kind of person you want to be or the personality you want to project.

Identify the first step

Powerful communication—the STEPP method

To help you work through the other steps suggested in this book, here are some guidelines and questionnaires.

1   WHO AM I?

* What sort of personality do I have?
* How do other people see me?
* What can I do to improve those aspects of my personality that I don't like?
* What new ways of behaving can I try out?
* Is my assessment of my self-image accurate or distorted?

Remember:

* People mirror your behaviour.
* The more depressed you get, the more people tend to accept your own assessment of yourself.
* Mistakes are okay. That's how we learn.
* Keep away from negative people and situations.
* A positive outlook attracts people.

2 HOW TO BUILD A POSITIVE SELF-IMAGE

Become an actor

★ Act the part of the person you want to be, *but*

★ Build on your own strengths, skills, talents *and*

★ Adopt what is comfortable for you. Don't parody others. Your desired image has to blend with your own personality and self-image.

Decide the area you need to work on

Consider the following questions:

★ How do you think others see you?

★ How do others appear to value you?

★ How much do you value yourself?

Write letters describing yourself from the point of view of:

★ your spouse

★ your best friend

★ your worst enemy

★ your boss

★ your child

★ your neighbour

★ someone you have helped.

Areas to change

Fill in the following chart to help you pinpoint areas you want to change:

Area	Your strengths	Your weaknesses
Your appearance: clothes and grooming		
Your attitude to work		
Your career choice		
Your relationships with your family		
Your relationships at work		
Your social relationships		
Your own general attitude to life		
Your continuing education (hobbies or career)		
Other		

Your life

Answer 'yes' or 'no 'to the following questions. (Occasionally the answer in your mind might be 'sometimes' rather than a definite 'yes' or 'no'. That's okay. The aim here is not to keep score, but to provide a basis for looking at yourself and what might have contributed to making you the person you are.)

1   Did you feel, as a child, that you didn't 'measure up' to parental expectations?

2   Were you ridiculed for being weaker/thinner/fatter/less intelligent/less attractive than others?

3   Were your parents abusive/alcoholic?

4   Were you spoilt as a child, accustomed to getting everything you wanted without effort on your part?

5   Do you feel you have achieved success:
    * at work?
    * in relationships?
    ★ as a parent?

6   Can you name any action you can take to improve your performance:
    * at work?
    * in relationships?
    * as a parent?

7   Can you name one self-defeating habit you have?

8   Can you name one achievement you're proud of?

9   Do you have a special skill/talent?

10   Have you developed or nurtured this skill/talent?

11   Is there something you would really like to achieve in this life?

12   Can you take a step towards achieving that goal now?

13   Can you think of one way in which you can help others?

14   Has anyone ever asked for your help or guidance?

15   Do you ever take time at the beginning of a day to think about what you want to achieve in that day?

16   Are you letting negative feelings about yourself, your job, or your relationships keep you trapped?

17   Do you have a balance in your life between work and play?

18   Do you feel you have real choices in life?

Now look over your answers.

What do they tell you about yourself?

What areas of your life are you happy with?

Are there any changes you want to make?

Your appearance

Consider the following aspects of your appearance:

1   Your body

★   Does your posture show confidence or defeat?

★   Are you healthy enough to radiate energy, attractiveness and a positive attitude?

★   Does your facial expression communicate confidence and contentment or negativity and dissatisfaction?

2   Your grooming

★   Does your general appearance reflect a style that suits you—hair, clothes and make-up?

★   Are your clothes:

–   neat?

–   clean?

–   ironed?

–   fashionable (not extreme)?

–   appropriate for the occasion?

–   comfortable?

3   HOW TO COMMUNICATE WITH OTHERS

Talking with others

★   Make eye contact.

★   Speak first.

★   Be friendly.

★   Listen.

★   Speak slowly.

★   Ask questions.

★ Be interesting:
 – Cultivate wide interests: books, newspapers, films, performances, videos, travel, sport, health.
★ Be empathetic:
 – People become much more receptive to you and your ideas if they have had a chance to express themselves first.
 – Everyone is interesting in some way. Find out what it is for everyone you meet.

Speaking to groups

★ Words are a tool: you can use them skilfully or poorly.
★ Verbal communication is self-expression: you reflect your own attitudes and values every time you speak.
★ To be an effective communicator, you must strive to transmit your *intended* meaning to other people.
★ You need to engage the emotions of your listeners.
★ Effective speaking is a way of satisfying our needs.
★ If you become confident in your ability to express yourself in any situation—social, business, or personal—then you are more likely to meet with success in all your relationships.
★ Always remember to speak to the level of your audience.

Whenever you feel nervous, just remind yourself to stop worrying about the impression you are making and consider how the other person is feeling. And remember, the same rules apply for effective conversationalists as for effective speakers.

4   EFFECTIVE PUBLIC SPEAKING

The four myths

If you're nervous about 'having a go' at public speaking, remember that the following fears are nothing but myths:

★ Some people are natural speakers.
★ Nerves are uncontrollable.
★ I'll forget what I was going to say!
★ I'll make a fool of myself.

Planning your speech

If you want to give a successful speech, then plan, plan, plan! Just sit down and carefully consider these two essential points:

* What is the intention of my speech?
    - to thank
    - to inform
    - to motivate
* Who is the audience?

Structure of your speech

When the big day comes and you have to face the fact that you really will be giving a speech, just remember that all speeches have the same basic structure. Don't be afraid. Think of all the hard work you have put in to get to this point. You've come a long way. Many people never have spoken and never will speak in public. Be proud of how much you have achieved to get this far. Remember the structure of a speech:

* introduction (ABC technique)
* body (keep it local, keep it simple, identify with the audience)
* conclusion (leave listeners with a lasting impression, tie things up).

Don't forget the 'easybuild' technique

The 'easybuild' technique really makes the job so much simpler. When you've worked out this technique and used it successfully, and you've learnt about self-confidence and how to project a positive self-image: *help someone else do it too.* Not only will they be eternally grateful, but your own self-esteem will rise even more because *you* have the power to help someone else. Now … remember the 'easybuild' technique?

* brainstorm
* the IBC pages
* draft.

Checklist for speech-building

* Open with an easy, warm introduction.
* Lead slowly and logically into your presentation.
* Reinforce your views with facts and reasons.

* Have a definite message and present it clearly.
* Close with a positive statement.

By this stage, you're probably feeling pretty good about yourself. And so you should be. Sometimes, the last part—being an effective communicator in writing—can seem rather daunting. Many, many people don't write unless they absolutely have to. But you have come so far, and learnt so much. Is it really so hard to master the last little step?

The key to being an effective communicator in writing is, like anything else, largely a matter of three things: confidence, determination and practice.

Practise writing a little every day (a journal is a good way of doing this). Soon you will have just as much confidence about your writing skills as you do all the other areas in which you have honed your skills.

5 EFFECTIVE WRITING

Why people find writing difficult

* It's difficult to express shades of meaning.
* It's difficult to sound like yourself.
* Once words are on paper they're more permanent.
* You don't know how other people will react to them.
* It takes a long time to write, rewrite, juggle sentences to express yourself, redraft and so on.
* You don't know what other people expect.

Some simple rules for writing

* Know your audience.
* Know what you want to say about your subject.
* Know how you're going to say it (explain, compare, describe etc.).
* Keep related points together.
* Write in plain English.
* Don't use words you don't understand.
* Avoid the use of jargon or 'in' words.

And remember, if you can't write well, or don't have time to write, hire someone who can do it for you.

SCHOOL IS NEVER OUT

I will leave you with a final thought. If you want to continue being an interesting and interested person as you go through life—a person who finds doors opening wherever you go, whatever you want to do—*never, never stop learning.*

There are always fascinating new discoveries, new ways of tackling problems and new ways of thinking about things. You owe it to yourself, as someone highly skilled in relating to others, to keep nourishing your mind.

Stay fit.

Stay keen.

Stay interested.

Stay a winner—*keep learning.*